CHI-SAO

THE GENIUS OF WING CHUN

JASON KOROL

To Sifu Tony who has taught me, inspired me, and shown through the years the true heart of a Sifu. None of my Wing Chun books are possible without you and I hope they honor you, bless our Wing Chun family, and inspire and inform the next generation. Such has been your wish all along and I hope and pray I've contributed to that in some way. You are that rarest of men and teachers: someone who genuinely, and with his whole heart, wants his students better than him. In a world of ego and selfish ambition, you shine as an example of Christ-like character, faithfulness, and giving.

Me and the best Sifu a fella can have.

My Sifu with Grandmaster Ip Ching in front of Ip Man's Mook Jong.

Also, all of us owe a great debt to our ancestors who paved the way for us to be doing this amazing art. Without their skill and dedication we wouldn't know Wing Chun at all, right? This is especially the case with Grandmaster Ip Man. In an age of boasting, he was a very humble man who never called attention to himself. Also, he endured quite a bit of tumult and suffering in his life (Japanese invasion and occupation, the resulting loss of his property and income, the Maoist commies running him out of his homeland, etc.). We live in an age of whining and entitlement. Over against all that, Ip Man was never given to self-pity. Instead, he poured his knowledge and skill into others who have, in turn, passed along to us what they've learned. Though I never crossed hands with him personally, I stand on the shoulders of men he lifted up. It's always that way.

With that said, please allow me to extend my most heartfelt thanks and gratitude for the late master's work. I've been adopted into a deep and rich and glorious martial family. Any of us who learn the martial arts has that *connection to the past - to warrior/scholars who condescended to teach us when we knew nothing. In our time of vanity and self-absorption I pray that I continue to bring honor to all those who walked this path before me, guided me, and left signs so that I might not go astray.*

The very humble Ip Man. His teaching, passed down by his son (and others), along to my Sifu, through which I've learned Wing Chun and have the privilege and honor of sharing with you, the reader.

The world breaks everyone and afterward many are strong at the broken places. But those that will not break it kills. It kills the very good and the very gentle and the very brave impartially. If you are none of these you can be sure it will kill you too but there will be no special hurry."

— ERNEST HEMINGWAY, A FAREWELL TO ARMS

INTRODUCTION

Imagine reporting for basic training in the Army or Marines. A bunch of stuff would transpire that you'd rather expect. The eclectic hair-style options, the exotic array of fashion choices, the delectable culinary offerings, and, of course, those gracious hosts known as DI's. But seriously, what you wouldn't expect, nor would any working military ever do, is send you off to a scrimmage. And by that we mean a live-fire competition.

As I write this, in fact, my son's baseball team is gearing up for the start of its season by playing intra-squad scrimmages. MLB uses Spring Training much this way, and that's what pre-season football is basically - actual games that don't count. They're for practice and the practice is as close to the real thing as you can get.

The military can't do that, however, and for quite conspicuous reasons. We're talking about the military here, so don't think some jokers haven't already seriously contemplated this as a workable option for improving combat readiness. We know they have. They're always looking at ways to maximize the performance of their troops. To that end, everything involved in military training is (at least on paper) supposed to serve the purpose of preparing soldiers for war. Marching, getting up at the crack of the crack of dawn, standing at attention...all of that is *indirectly* about killing an enemy and breaking his toys. Those things inculcate the habits of character and self-control that assist a soldier in achieving war's primary goal.

But an actual scrimmage?

That would be insane.

It's for this reason that honest-to-goodness martial art training is more like military training than it is sport fighting. Military discipline intends to make soldiers who can control themselves, follow orders, know their weapons, and have seasoned "combative reflexes" through thousands of reps. This isn't any different than a martial artist in principle. Military training, due to the unpredictability and variations of war, can't become as hyper-focused on only one line of engagement as, say, a boxer can. There are vast differences between fighting in an urban center against irregular forces, duking it out in the desert versus another mechanized army with close-air support, and jungle warfare.

That's not much different than not knowing if you'll have to engage an enemy (or enemies) in the entry way of your home, a parking lot, or a public restroom - just to name a few. For these reasons, much training goes into building up attributes of body and character as well as "reflexive principles."

And this is where Chi-sao comes in.

Chi-sao isn't fighting. Rather, it's about developing and making precise certain reflexes needed to be successful at close-range in that veritable no-man's land between full-on striking and wrestling. Like a scrimmage in war, a live-fire drill where the participants exchange eye-gouges, elbows, hits to the neck, throat, and jaw, is as safe as driving with your eyes closed (though, in all honesty, that couldn't impair the drivers in my area more than they already are...just saying).

Chi-sao is a war-game. It's a pressure-test in which we take the structures developed in the empty hand forms and learn how they're applied. It teaches through pressure tests because learning war lessons in war is dangerously stupid stuff. Experience is indeed a brutal teacher, giving us the test first and the lesson later. Chi-sao, done right, saves us from too much guessing. It's a laboratory and classroom. It's philosophical - a conceptual bridge between the purely theoretical and the *potential of the application systematic* taught and implied in the forms. It's also stunningly practical - honing our skill to apply both the *lat sau jik chung* and *lin siu daai da* concepts of Wing Chun. We're taught to attack aggressively when there's an opening (the former) but to do so with defensive control (the latter concept). It's in Chi-sao drilling that this is best experienced.

Without Chi-sao there really is no Wing Chun. How else can we drill the essential components of the system's applications? How else can we bridge the gap between the theory of lat sau jik chung (when free of obstruction, attack instinctively) and its practice? How do we know for certain that our personal practice of lin siu daai da (simultaneous attack and defense) is skillful unless we practice it (safely) under pressure?

You see, Wing Chun's major principles are all best experienced during Chi-sao. Centerline, facing, stealing/borrowing power, and structural power from the ground up, are all best - and safely - trained in *the drill*. All-out fighting is far too dangerous to practice. And even if we tried there would still be conditions upon which we couldn't count in other engagements. All training requires some concessions - even if we were to ignorantly say there are none and let students have at it. There are always fences around our disciplines because we, being human, live within a world of fences both moral and physical. This means our choices of training should be as logical as possible in order to produce the results we want while minimizing risks to health as much a possible too.

Chi-sao does this. If we do it right. In this book we'll unpack what it means to "do it right" and the author's intent is to explain the amazing world of principled-pragmatism in which Chi-sao lives and breathes. You'll see how so very often people say things like *mind and body* and yet rarely take the time to unpack what that means. What does it mean in theory and practice - and what does it tell us about ourselves and the world around us? Real Wing Chun is a system of mind-body. It's a frightful tool and yet an exquisite one too; both shank and scalpel. A fearful and wonderfully made systematic that awes the mind and protects the body - from others and self! The genius of Wing Chun is seen ever so clearly in Chi-sao - it's a marvelous thing of sweet paradoxes that develops amazing power and speed upon a foundation of relaxation and logical structure. It's simple, yet comprehensive. It's furiously aggressive and yet calm and composed; it's deadly and serene. Indeed, there's nothing else like it and it's the glue that binds together our beloved Wing Chun.

So, come and be amazed with me as we explore the heart and soul of Wing Chun's heart and soul.

1

WHY CHI-SAO

"*All men seek happiness. This is without exception. Whatever different means they use, they all tend to this end. The cause of some going to war, and of others avoiding it, is the same desire in both - to be happy. This is the motive of every action of every man, even of those who hang themselves.*" *Blaise Pascal*

SURELY THIS IS true - and surely there are various means of achieving happiness, right? For a man who loves sports, going to the theatre isn't his first choice of having a good time. He prefers going to the ballgame. But neither choice, be sure, is evil. A ballgame is fine and, for that matter, so is going to a play. It's simply a question of preference, right? Both sports and theatre are acceptable means of entertainment in the whole realm of the pursuit of happiness thing.

But we're talking about self-defense and that narrows the option field a wee bit, doesn't it? One simply can't just go out and do any old thing when it comes to the field of violence. The pursuit of happiness differs vastly from self-defense in that the issue is no longer one of preference but hard and nasty necessity. That said, there's still some room for personal opinion. Let's get that out of the way. To say that Wing Chun is a valid science/logic of self-defense isn't to say that no other methodology will work. To suggest such is to throw the author's credibility to the wind, so we'll do no such thing. On the contrary, we're just making the case that Wing Chun is a *very* logical means of achieving the goal of self-defense and not the only one.

At Falls Park in downtown Greenville, South Carolina working with
Sifu Tony years ago.

A chair to the head is one way of getting the job done. Using a handgun or a knife...or even throwing your mother-in-law in the way and then running off. Those are all valid methods of defending oneself (that's assuming that your mother-in-law tactic won't put you in mortal danger with your wife). And surely, boxing or MMA training would be useful as well. No...in saying that Wing Chun is a valid science of self-defense we aren't claiming that nothing else has any use. In point of fact, the claim is that Wing Chun is a systematic that can be applied to the whole of the issue rather than mere parts.

If one has no chair, gun, knife, or that nagging in-law at their disposal, they're thrust upon the hard reality that it's their skill alone that stands between life and death. Indeed, if one's empty hand skills are all that stands between safety and that ruthless tyranny of assault, and that assault might take place in a variety of places, then Wing Chun is, in this author's opinion, quite practical. If every part of one's body is both a target and potential weapon and we're talking about no rule other than the jungle rule of survival, then we're talking about martial art. This much needs to be clear. And to that end it must also be clear what's not being said, which is that sport fighting methods like boxing are, despite their limits, indeed helpful reference points to the issue at hand. The effective fighting systems of our time often have their origin in the wars of that old jungle - of days of anarchy and strife. They are often domesticated as men and women become convinced that life-or-death is a predicament of the past... you know, in an unenlightened age before Netflix and Google.

To this we must say that a martial art isn't a safe thing, though it must be trained safely. On the contrary, it's a wild and dangerous thing. Wing Chun, being a true war-art, a martial art, is like that. It's a loaded gun, which must be handled safely. Training with a firearm is a specific thing, after all. One simply doesn't go off half-cocked, firing willy-nilly at any target one fancies. That's an easy way to end up in jail, right?

So, keeping with the firearm analogy, let's say that Wing Chun is the Glock of firearms. It's not for use at 300 yards. Of course, one can try that, but there are better weapons for that range. The Glock is best deployed at extremely close range and so is Wing Chun. Get where we're going with this? The whole thing is context. And this brings us to the subject at hand. The idea of Wing Chun is to use offense as defense and defense as offense. The goal is all-in-one. As you'll see, when not at a distance kicking or punching, which is what we may call *sporting range*, Wing Chun provides us tools to simultaneously disrupt the enemy's balance and attack their command-and-control center.

This is to say their head and neck.

And by attack we don't mean gentle taps and smacks. This is violent business.

Get their head, neck, throat with non-contradictory structure (mechanics developed through forms and drills) and simultaneously take their balance. Everything else that happens is in service to this primary objective.

But saying something and doing it aren't the same thing. Everything requires training so as to make sure the proper technique is deployed without contradiction. Eye-gouges and smashing some evil dude's noggin into countertops and/or walls actually requires training drills to make these things automatic.

Chi-sao is that training drill.

The forms give us the raw mechanical material used in the drill. And this is where the Glock/Wing Chun analogy breaks down because when we purchase a firearm we literally have the weapon and the question is now how to use it. Don't miss this. The forms and drills of Wing Chun are taking us to the factory to *make the weapon*. On the side of a Glock it reads: Austria. If we in Wing Chun were so branded it would say, *Siu Lim Tao, Chum Kiu, Biu Jee, Mook Jong*, and Chi-sao. Such is the factory that makes the weapon we become.

(This is also to say that tactics - how to use the weapon - are another, though interrelated, subject.)

A few things to say about it right off the bat to assist us in avoiding trouble.

First, yes, we need forms to produce optimum mechanical skill and then a progressive drill in which we learn to use those mechanics. Skill never comes unless skillful reflexes are trained against reasonable resistance.

Second, the drill - especially considering the danger of the targets - must have built in safety mechanisms or else it's barbarism, not martial arts. One of the great merits of Chi-sao is that it provides the ability to hone the neuromuscular reflexes to get at those targets without defensive compromise.

Third, the trainees must start with sound technique. Kindergarten is the "momma-poppa" phase of rolling hands that you see all that time. It's the grammar school of infighting that calibrates those fundamental mechanics learned in the forms. To skip this phase for any reason is like sending a child straight to grad-school.

Fourth, we're supposed to go to grad-school. It's a mistake to stay in 1st grade, always doing Chi-sao according to the "rules" and only with others who play by those rules. Chi-sao fundamentals should yield the fruit of infighting skill to be used, without contradiction, in any manner necessary. Wrestlers are good at "hand-fighting" within the rules of their sport. Likewise, good Chi-sao should provide the ability to hand-fight with any wrestler, or to clinch with any boxer, and dominate due to Wing Chun's logically superior systematic (in regard to all-out fighting, that is). This will not happen if Wing Chun students only use Chi-sao against other Wing Chun students in the grammar school positions. We see the results of this time and again as Wing Chun adherents display an almost comical misunderstanding of true fighting. Chi-sao brings us to grad-school in a variety of ways...dealing with heavy pressing energy, dealing with grapplers who change levels, or with those who disengage in order to swing. Not only that, transitions to locking, throwing, and breaking too! Very few people, sadly, get the most of of Wing Chun because of the misapprehension of Chi-sao.

FIFTH, we must not confuse the drill for fighting. We are not, repeat not, trying to stand straight in front of someone and gaining contact at the fore-arms. That's the drill, the start of it anyway, not the application reality. A drill is a specific segment of reality, isolated for training and safety purposes, with the intent to develop necessary skill so as to overcome the challenge presented by that reality.

Drills like Chi-sao are, therefore, needed and yet dangerous. Needed because reality must be adjusted to and dealt with; the real world accommodates no man. With no apology to Protagoras, man is not the measure of all things. And it's dangerous because the technical specifics of the drill can too often become the *goal* of the training rather than the reality that's supposed to be its measure.

Sixth, like with the empty hand forms, an advanced student still goes back to the basics of Chi-sao in order to make sure his/her fundamentals are not decaying. Though we're not to stay in grammar school we still use good grammar. And because of the real possibility of bad habits creeping in, we should be vigilant.

Seventh, no other system offers the infighting self-defender such a logical drill. This means that Wing Chun's Chi-sao is the key to avoiding the pitfalls of over-reliance on sport technique on the inside, or dead patterns that lack the ability to adapt and overcome spirited resistance by the enemy.

Eighth, the Wing Chun student, as mentioned previously, must learn the critical distinction between technical skill, drills, and application tactics. Certainly, they're all related and are meant to run together. It may be bold to say but is probably true that nearly all the problems of Wing Chun today stem from a breakdown of this philosophical chain. We'll discuss this throughout the book for the purposes of trying to clear away some of the debris cluttering our minds.

The complete Wing Chun student is, therefore, an athlete, a technician, and *Art of War* student. They're in very good physical condition, both for combat's sake and for general morality (one should care for the gift of life they've been given and not abuse it by unhealthy habits). They take special care of their own technical development and study the forms with respect and diligence because neglect of the body, just like with a garden, leads to disarray. And they're a scholar too. Sun Tzu's classic work should be studied. Any martial art student who doesn't pay attention to fighting tactics and the absolute necessity of having an edge (in order to avoid a pitched battle of give and take) is less than half of what they could be. An ignoramus may be a Wing Chun student, but he'll never be a good one. Success in every field requires focused effort and in Wing Chun this is doubly true. Technical skill and drilling competence alone are insufficient. Together they form half of the Wing Chun student's actual ability insofar as self-defense application is concerned. Unless we invest ourselves in proper tactical theory we're like a body without a mind.

And then, finally, and only then, we're philosophers of the fist because we've arrived at systematic integration.

2

BASICS OF THE DRILL

I t's true that there's no way to teach Chi-sao through a book. That will require you having to actually cross hands with a skilled practitioner and coach/Sifu. The thing is, though, a book can give you a missing ingredient insofar as the heart and soul of the exercise is concerned. By providing the big picture of it all, that is to say, the primary goal of it, we can certainly use a book to point the practitioner in the right direction.

In this chapter we go over some of the basic movements of our Chi-sao curriculum. It's true, you can't feel the pressure and gauge the reactions via the printed page. What you can do, however, is use this chapter, the photos and descriptions - especially the latter - to hone in on the heart and soul of the drill. Remember, the drill isn't the goal but is used to achieve the goal of non-contradictory infighting skill. Many people make errors of extremes (a great plague in our thinking) and either over-simplify close-quarter combat or make Chi-sao into a hyper-technical game of hand-chasing. The former eschew the drill altogether and rely on various forms of simplified and non-reactionary drills. The latter turn Chi-sao into a set-piece battle only applicable to Wing Chun fighters rather than seeing it as a gateway to fight all fighters, via structural principles and pressure testing.

Basic starting position is right arm Bong when in top position and Taan in low position. Bong/Taan is defending the flank, so to speak, from the riding/cover hand cutting across to your middle. Therefore, the inside hand (Bong/Taan) energy is flowing toward the shoulder. The left arm is in Fook-Sao position and it flows toward the center of mass. This is the critical thing to know about the basic hand positions. Think of them as "inside and outside" hands. The outside hand, if not directed toward the center, will leave your middle wide open. The opposite is true for your inside hand. This is the main defensive idea of Chi-sao.

The main idea of basic "rolling" is to develop the core characteristics of scientific in-fighting. These positions are not absolutely necessary for fighting success but the principles they convey, and the energy/force used are.

The rolling action is not circular but, rather, a mutually offsetting forward pressure applied by both parties. Aaron's fook-sao is guarding his center against my Taan/Bong and vice versa. Our hands do not, repeat not, have to be on the center, but they must control it. Like a guard can be outside the building he's guarding, the seed hands (Fook, Taan, Bong) guard the center and flank. The technique should be springy and fluid. To achieve this skill, start with "zero energy" to overcome your natural stiffness. Rushing through the zero energy phase will damage your ability to achieve skill later on. Stiffness is your mortal enemy as it robs you of the ability to react quickly to your enemy. Don't rush through the zero-energy phase, nor neglect touching base with it as your progress. If you skip this and/or don't maintain practice of it, you'll soon find that you're unable to advance.

Many students rush through this section of Chi-sao, eager, of course, to start learning to strike. But the issue isn't the striking. It's the positional control and proper use of energy/force; it's using proper technique to cut off your partner's access to your center-of-mass while simultaneously "flowing" toward his. Continue to do "poon-sao" rolling without striking or heavy force until your hands develop a natural springiness in them. The *"laat sau jik chung"* principle is being trained in earnest, which is that your hands aren't seeking their hands, but to attack when free of obstruction. Moreover, and not to be missed, you're also developing the *"lin siu daai da"* principle of simultaneous attack and defense. Defense is of critical importance or else everything we're learning (and the rest of this book) is superfluous. At this phase of your training you want to pay careful attention to developing fluid structure. Make sure that your Fook-sao isn't too "heavy" and that your Taan isn't going past the shoulder line, etc.

Even after you move on and develop more skill and acquire striking and locking ability, it's a good idea to come back to Poon-sao to check "your energy" and make sure bad habits aren't creeping in. Mastery of the basic positions while rolling gives you control and that's the key to the whole shebang. No other fighting system provides such a brilliant drill as this. When done properly it trains us to attack the enemy's "general" (their head, eyes, jaw, neck, throat), take their balance, and do so without contradiction. This gives us the ability to be very violent...logically and with consummate control. Chi-sao, done right, is grappling for the attack and control of the "general."

Once you get the hang of this, both parties should start using light force and footwork. This will help your structure immensely. When doing this, make sure you maintain facing and relaxed, springy technique. Never fight force with force. Stay in your basic training stance.

Pressure Drill

The goal in the pressure drill is for the students to maintain good, relaxed structure when rolling. Don't start this drill until you've achieved reasonable skill at the basic rolling. Once that's set, one partner can step forward using the basic advancing step. The advancing partner isn't trying to strike at this point. He's merely using his structure and adding footwork. The defensive partner will be forced to step back if the advance is done with both the footwork and upper body connected. The idea is to step back at an angle (using Tiu Ma footwork) or a slight pivot. This will create an angle through which the defensive person can strike. Skipping this drill, or as many do, underestimating its value, will likely cause you to "chase hands" (the dreaded disease of Wing Chun) and think that technique is more important than positioning. In fact, the better your shifting and stepping is integrated into your basic structure, the less you have to move your hands to both cover and attack.

Elliot and I start rolling using the basic hand positions.

To do the pressure drill both parties should have good fundamentals. At this point we're using springy energy and watching our technique.

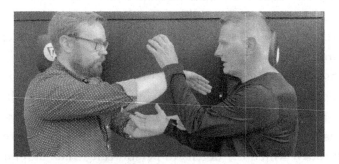

At this point, though, I begin to press forward against Elliot's Bong-sao. His basic structure is good enough to hold the line but under heavy pressure he "lets me help him hurt me" by shifting. My pressure, as you'll see in the next photo, will cause me to lurch forward into his counter-strike once he releases the line.

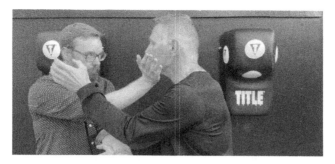

Elliot's shift allows him access to my middle. It's the essence of not fighting force with force. Many novices mistakenly think that Chi-sao is a game of fancy hand techniques but as you see here it's really about handling pressure with the basics. Elliot's technical integration is the key...his stance, structure, and footwork/shifting allows him to exploit improper use of energy. To the untrained eye, it might even look like he didn't do much at all...just knocked me out with a nasty palm strike under the chin.

DOING the pressure drill is an easily overlooked part of Chi-sao training that teaches the proper use of structure, facing, and simplicity. The erroneous belief, as mentioned in the last photo's caption, is that Chi-sao is all about hand techniques and flashiness. In fact, it's about good structure (springy power) and footwork/shifting. Remember: no matter how good your hand techniques are, if you can't move with them, are useless in fighting. Those who put the necessary time into this relatively simple drill will overcome the common problem of too much tension in their arms and fighting force with force. In these photos we demonstrate attacks most common from the angles created by good Wing Chun structure and footwork. However, the key isn't striking. The goal of the drill is to learn to use springy pressure and learn to react to the enemy's attack - soft, yet not yielding; firm, yet not stiff. It's a delicate balance that takes time and focus. The ability to use all of your strength and speed, with good form, without being stiff, and while reading/reacting to your enemy is the key to Wing Chun in-fighting and goal of Chi-sao practice.

In this photo I've countered Aaron's forward pressure by angling to the side and punching. If someone is pressing too hard, don't fight force with force. Shift or step to the angle instead. This is the benefit of doing Poon-sao properly. As Aaron pressured forward, I let go of my Bong-sao and used the angle to strike with my left hand. At this point I'm in a very strong position to follow up with more attacks. Many families teach that you should always be straight in front of the enemy but this is a flawed premise. The better your footwork and shifting, the less risk you take with complex hand motions. Simplicity is key. You don't want your enemy able to directly face you when you attack.

Good structure of your stance and arm position allows you to use footwork and shifting to both dissolve attacks AND counter. This is the heart of soul of simultaneous attack and defense. At this point, I want to take Aaron's balance while following up lest he turn and we get into a fire-fight. ALWAYS take their balance once you get the superior position. This is the principle of Chiu Ying-Bi Ying...of not letting your enemy face you on the inside. It's the core of successful infighting. We only stand straight in front of one another as a form of neutrality for training purposes.

The Wing Chun "butterfly palms" are explosive pushing actions that have a snappy strike aspect. Don't underestimate how important the palms are in off-balancing your enemy in cluttered environments.

One of the things that's overlooked about the efficacy of grappling systems is that on the inside, the grappler is able to smother his enemy's ability to strike. Smothering and control of balance are first in the order of business in BJJ and even, with the neck/head control of Muay Thai. Wing Chun is actually no different. It just can't ignore the strikes to soft targets, so its structural system is different. The principle is the same, though.

The last thing in the world you want is to be at extreme close-range with someone who has their balance. I can't scream this loud enough: there is no way to control all their actions at full speed if they have their balance. That's why we want to close off our center when facing and take the flank and balance when possible. Good Poon-sao will teach you to shut down the centerline attacks, control their striking and grabbing attempts, and use pivots, shifts, and small angle steps to defend and attack.

In this photo you see the angle created by my shifting to the outside as Aaron tried to overpower me. Good defense will yield offensive opportunities if you're patient and let your enemy help you hit him. This is what it means to use his aggression against him. Poon-sao and shifting/stepping while keeping your structure will open a new and incredible world to you. You'll see that the strikes take care of themselves. Instead of standing straight in front of your enemy trying to finagle a way through his arms, thinking that's Wing Chun, you'll instead use good structure against his pressure to create positional advantages. Later, it will also teach you to use your own attacking pressure to create attack angles.

In this case Elliot responds to my pressure by shifting the other way and then releasing the Bong-sao. The shifting Bong (Yi-Bong) in the Chum Kiu form provides the best technical foundation for this move but here is the application. When there's too much force coming forward, shift and allow the excess pressure to release.

After shifting and letting go of his Bong-sao, Elliot uses a straight punch to yours truly. We all know this is just training and no one could ever actually hit me. After these photos were taken, in fact, I pummeled him mercilessly so he didn't get a big head. He cried for a while but he's okay. Just saying.

Okay, seriously though, here's the same pressure from the other angle with Elliot doing the press. A slight step forward with the pressure is a good way to go rather than having your upper body lean in. In this case, because Elliot steps in, I had to slide my right foot slightly to make sure the shift gave me enough room.

After releasing my Bong-sao and getting the angle, Elliot blocks my punch.

But because I have the better position I don't need to shift or step. Instead, I step forward and execute a Paak-sao and neck strike. The Paak and step cause Elliot to lose his balance and structure, which gives me more safety via control. Take a good look at this position and let it sink in. Good Wing Chun/in-fighting is contingent upon control and position. A good many students are taught not to push, pull, or move during the drill. They're taught that doing so is bad Wing Chun. But that's exactly what the drill teaches us to handle. No one is going to stand straight in front of us using "zero-energy" and/or "proper" Chi-sao hands. Doing the pressure drill will being to open the door to real-world application by teaching you how good structure and footwork interact with heavy pressure. As you get more seasoned, your partner should be able to really press forward at any moment. Despite the uncertainty of the timing and the pressure, good training will yield highly efficient and explosive, springy force for you.

ONCE YOU HAVE the hang of Poon-sao with pressure, it's time to focus on the common striking techniques. Now, we note that this is all integrated, not some form of slap-dash nonsense where we're piling more and more technical detail into our training. Doing this makes us martial hoarders, not Kung-fu men/women.

The attacks are based on the structural defense built into the Wing Chun system. Without the Yi Ji Kim Yeung Ma, there's no Siu Lim Tao. And without SLT, there's no Chi-sao structure. And without that structure that uses the YJKYM and Chum Kiu, there's no shifting or stepping. And without shifting or stepping, there's no positional control. This is the "golden chain" of the Wing Chun Kuen *Sum Faat* (or, in other words, the heart law of the Wing Chun fistic system). The strikes and techniques are basic and obvious and flow from the positional advantage of one's structure and footwork. Misapprehension of this chain of fistic logic will eviscerate our Wing Chun if we're not careful.

INSIDE HAND/TAAN-SAO Attack

Use the basic rolling positions to learn the basic attacks.

In this case, Aaron is going to step forward and apply pressure. It works the same if I step forward.

As he does this, by holding my position it creates an opening in which my Taan-sao hand can shoot forward. In this case I use a side palm (Juk Jeung). This is a common "inside" attack from our Taan hand. When combined with the footwork of your opponent stepping in, or your own as you cut him off (using Jeet Ma), it's a dreadful blow. It catches the enemy right on the jaw.

This simple attack is devastating once you get the hang of it. In good Wing Chun we eschew useless and vain games of "gotcha" or "tag." You'll notice that I have my full structural weight at my disposal and still control the middle line with my non-striking arm. By stepping forward with my attack and following through, this is a frightful tool. It looks so basic that many people overlook its importance in in-fighting.

In more advanced Chi-sao, there's no "momma-poppa" rolling. You simply cross hands more like you would in a fight (clinch or tie-ups happen often). The "rolling" action is no longer confined to right/left...it goes in any direction, in fact. In this photo notice how Aaron catches Devin with the same strike but from the left hand. The inside or Taan-sao attack can be a palm, or even an eye-gouge. The issue is that it "rides" the corner toward the target without giving up control of the enemy's outside arm. Again, combined with footwork and follow-ups, this simple attack is devastating. It's so effective exactly because you've taken the time to learn springy control during the Poon-sao and pressure phase.

Here's Rob smacking the bejabbers out of David using the palm strike. Rob used his footwork to avoid David's aggression, which carried the latter offline and exposed him to this powerful strike.

COVER HAND/FOOK-SAO Attack

The second basic attack is from top/cover hand (Fook-sao). In this case, Aaron has the top/inside position closed off. It's a good idea not to try and force one's way through. If the line is closed, be patient. A common mistake is for the Wing Chun student to launch attacks willy-nilly. Remember: your first responsibility is control and defense. Getting into a shootout and exchanging fire isn't the point.

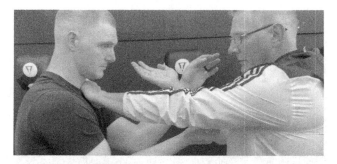

In this case, Aaron's inside hand comes too far into the center, which opens him to outside attack. Many novices will attack with their inside hand to the inside line, a mistake we're trained to avoid by proper use of the Taan-sao concept. I could use any number of strikes from this angle. In this case I use Faak-sao to the neck/throat while sure to cover the middle.

In this angle you can see how I've shifted slightly to fire the Faak-sao strike. This is an effective strike but must be used carefully (with proper angles) or Aaron can trade. By shifting to the side slightly, I have the ability to execute this strike, or any variation, at a slightly upward angle. This is important in case Aaron tried to grapple. In that case, he'd impale himself on the incoming strike by moving downward into its path. This is why Wing Chun structure is what it is and we shouldn't skip steps! Done properly, it effectively answers infighting questions like grabbing and wrestling as well as striking.

Here, Aaron is teaching Devin to use the Fook-sao/cover hand attack. Look at the angle Devin has and how the strike would whack Aaron right on the jaw. Yes, the eyes, throat and neck are soft targets, but so is the chin/jaw. Getting your jaw slammed by a side-palm will certainly rattle the old birdcage.

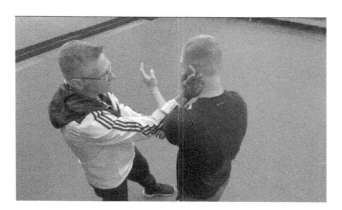

We can't teach you to actually Chi-sao in a book, of course. But we can certainly correct common misconceptions and point you in the right direction. Here, notice how my angle is very strong. Against overly aggressive opponents, good structure with footwork and stepping will give you these types of positions. Against Aaron's pressure, I used an angle-step and was able to attack from the outside using the Fook-sao structure. This is a result of using the Poon-sao pressure drill over and over. Like I said, if you master that, the attacks take care of themselves. If you skip that step, you'll try flashy stuff while standing in front of your enemy. Simple is best. Flashy is trashy.

Notice the total control Aaron has over Devin's structure and balance. If he was playing a game of "Gotcha" instead, then he'd be leaving himself open to tackles and haymakers. Resist the temptation to add "cool" techniques and stick to the basics. Infighting is about control; it's grappling with strikes, or striking with grappling (in this case, we mean pushing and pulling). We don't merely want to hit him but also control his balance and have a superior angle.

This is an example of more "freestyle" Chi-sao using the basic concepts. Notice that Aaron isn't limiting himself to hand-chasing or a rigid interpretation of keeping contact only at the forearm. He uses the Fook-sao concept to cover Devin's left hand while using the Taan-sao side attack. It's always control and hit.

Paak-sao Attack

The next attack that's common is the inside Paak-sao, which happens when Aaron is leaning a bit on his top hand. It's common for novices to press with one hand and forget the other one.

In this case, I use Paak-sao from my outside (Fook) hand to free up my top (Bong) hand.

The simultaneous Paak & Faak Sao, coupled with Aaron's leaning in/forward pressure, makes this almost as effective as a French guillotine. Okay, maybe not that bad, but you get the idea. Why would I use a Faak-sao rather than a side-palm or punch? It has to do with the angle and where the energy is moving. This is why Chi-sao is so important to the Wing Chun fighter as it trains us to reflexively attack openings in the most efficient and non-contradictory manner.

In this angle you can see how I've shifted a little to help secure the strike. Again, this is a blazing fast action that prevents the enemy from countering/trading. We want control with every hit. A hit that doesn't also prevent the enemy from grappling/charging us is dangerous. Losing this perspective has caused many Wing Chun families to lose ground to modern BJJ/MMA style fighting. Our striking is grappling and our grappling is striking! You can't see this in the photo but I'm stepping into the strike and pushing Aaron off balance all at once.

Bong-Sao/Lop Sao Attack

Again, we're back in the basic roll. If Aaron puts too much pressure on my Bong-sao (a common problem), I don't want to carry the weight. Below are the most common attacks possible due to his use of pressure.

If Aaron is using a lot of pressure that's aimed directly at me, I let my Bong-sao go. Remember, don't carry him on your Bong-sao. It's not made for that and will burn your shoulder out, possibly causing injury. With a slight shift in my YJKYM to the right, I fire a left punch/attack. Since Aaron's energy is directly at my center, my attack is blocked.

But his energy/force carries him into my Lop-Faak attack.

If his energy/force is moving toward my left shoulder, not my center, I can let my Bong go as I shift and punch. This is more direct. Notice again how Aaron is unable to face me directly. Step or shift only as much as needed. Novices have a tendency to over-do it and end up losing their ability to face. Remember: we want him off-facing, not both of us.

This angle shows the result of Aaron's overcommitment to the top line. By letting my Bong-sao go and shifting with the left attack, I have a very good angle to hit and control.

COVER HAND/FOOK-SAO Attacks

If your enemy's inside hand (the Taan-sao action) is collapsed, which is to say, it's not covering his flank, it opens the door for our Fook-sao hand to attack. This is a common error that you can take advantage of often if you master your basics.

In this case, because of the angle, I use Faak-sao but you may also deploy a Juk-jeung (side palm) to his jaw or even an eye-gouge while covering the middle. Again, the reason this attack is open is because Aaron has let his inside hand drift too far to the middle. The Taan-sao covers the flank. Fook beats Taan when Taan is in the middle. Taan beats Fook when Fook is on the shoulder.

I know this is a repeat photo but Aaron's teaching Devin the cover-hand attack from the other side so I wanted to point something out. Notice how Devin uses the palm strike rather than the Faak-sao and that his elbow is controlling the center. In our family we use the Faak-sao quite a bit but you must be careful that you don't open up your center. If you throw it too much like a back-hand chop, thereby raising the elbow, you can expose yourself to danger.

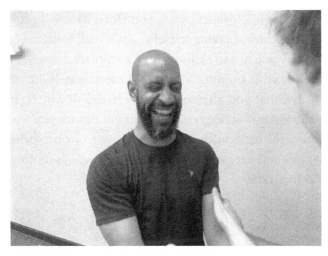

The look of a man who's beginning to get the hang of things. But seriously, we should be training hard and with appropriate focus and safety. Yes. But we should also be having fun and enjoying time with our Kung-fu brothers and sisters. If not, Chi-sao becomes a competition rather than a skill-building drill where we gain life-saving reflexes and overcome our natural mistakes such as tension and uneconomical movements.

HUEN-SAO ATTACKS

THE USE of Huen Sao is a game changer. It opens up a much more fluid and diverse approach to Chi-sao than is possible in a strict adherence to the "*momma-poppa*" approach. Don't get me wrong, it's essential that we get the basics but if we stay there we end up with a strictly Wing Chun vs. Wing Chun Chi-sao game that becomes so hyper-technical as to make it unusable against non-Wing Chun fighters. Huen-sao, on the other hand, by virtue of the ability to both control and change lines of engagement simultaneously allows you to adapt to whatever style you encounter. Though we'll show you a few uses of the circling hand in the following photos, be sure that they're virtually unlimited in use and, when added to shifting and footwork, bring your in-fighting skill to a very high level. More still, the footwork, shifting, angles, level-changes, and Huen-sao, will revolutionize your in-fighting game, making it useful against all forms of fighters. If you can't use your Chi-sao skills against grapplers, boxers, and Muay Thai infighters, your training has been, unfortunately, in vain. Make sure, as always, that you already have the basics down. Trying to use the Huen-sao against an aggressive opponent before you've mastered the pressure drill especially, and know how to exert springy-structural force, will end very much like a Dallas Cowboys football season: in tears and frustration.

While not flashy like some Chi-sao styles, the Huen-sao technique is the epitome of being like water. By mastering the ability to circle around heaviness, pressure, and tension, you'll learn to exploit your enemy's inability to change directions quickly.

Because Aaron was laying on my Taan-sao hand, I'm able to circle to the outside instead of fighting force with force. We should have the structural power to hold positions but not be tense. When Aaron is overcommitted to the line, my Huen-sao is able to "run" to the other side.

In this case, I quickly press with a Gum-sao/pinning hand and strike once I have the outside angle secured.

The follow-up comes fast and efficiently from the other hand (using the Faan-sao/repeating hand principle.

In this case, I used a circling hand and immediately rode the new outside position using the Fook-sao concept to deliver a strike down Aaron's center. The Huen-sao/circling hand is the ace-in-the-hole for the Wing Chun fighter who masters relaxed, springy pressure. Due to their inherent tension, people won't be able to keep up with your ability to change directions to dissolve force.

Here's another angle of the Huen-sao. Its effectiveness hinges on the proper read of Aaron's energy and exploits his overcommitment (usually due to tension) to a line. It's backed up by my ability to shift/step offline as I deploy the circling hand in case he tries to attack in the gap. The Huen-sao is practiced so often in the empty hand forms precisely because it's so essential an inside skill. It's a small and controlled action that doesn't expose our center.

*Circling hands can be used from either hand. As you see here, the right hand Huen-sao I used above created an angle of attack and control as Aaron's energy/force shifted him to away from my center. Practice these attacks slowly, smoothly, and without tension so that they become second nature. **They're the hallmark of our particular Ip Man Wing Chun family**...lots of shifting, small steps and attacks/pushes off of Huen-sao.*

In this sequence you'll notice that we aren't restrained by the "momma-poppa" roll. In real fighting, contact and clinches can happen in a variety of ways, so as your Chi-sao improves you're able to apply its principles without being bound by them in a legalistic fashion.

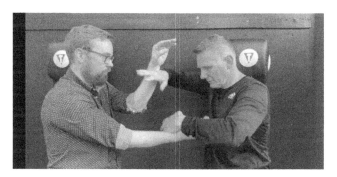

I begin to shift to my right, forming Bong-sao to cover the shifting angle, and using Huen-sao on the "weak side" that I'm vacating. This requires mastery of being able to use both hands independently, a key feature of good Wing Chun.

When the shift and circling hand are complete I now have access to the inside line. Note how I'm still controlling the high-line with the Yi-Bong action. My Huen-sao has freed my left hand for attack.

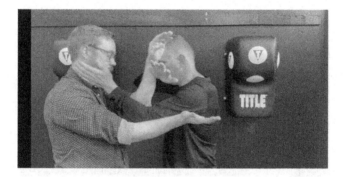

Go where there's emptiness. By not fighting force with force through coordinated shifting and circling actions, I step through the gap left in Elliot's defense and slam home a strike. The strike is contingent upon his reaction. In this case I use a side-palm. In other cases you might use a thumb to the eye using the Fook-sao structure. But, again, notice that I'm still controlling Elliot's left arm and my angle neutralizes his right.

Same high starting point.

This time I execute the "same" move, except that Elliot's energy is a little higher this time. This makes circling over the top more dangerous, if not impossible, so I switch and go under.

This shows how versatile the circling hand (Huen) is. If you can't go one way, the other must be open. No one is everywhere. The trick is learning the basics so well and staying relaxed in order to "be like water."

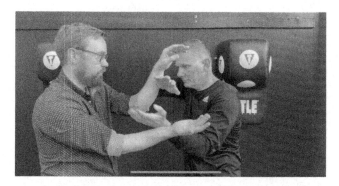

Whether over or under, I now have the inside line.

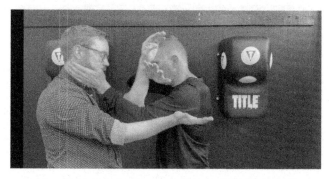

Though this photo happens in a sequence, it's all flowing and once I had the inside line I instantly stepped into the gap with the strike.

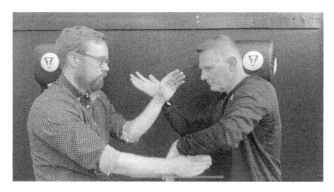

Another variation is that you'll notice that instead of holding the other line with a Bong-sao, I have contact at the wrist. Ultimately, our Chi-sao must move beyond the "momma-poppa" positions. Initially we make contact at the forearms in order to teach proper position, energy and gain technical experience. It's like teaching someone to drive. Both hands on the wheel and you stay out of heavy traffic, right? If we never pull out of the parking lot and onto the roadway, we aren't really driving. Chi-sao is the same way. To be used as it should - that is, against non-Wing Chun fighters - we must have the ability to "roll" from any position.

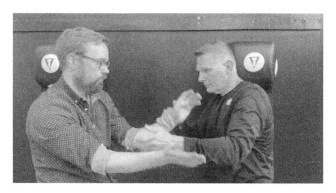

My left circling hand is doing the same thing as in the other photos but now I use my right to Jut-sao to yank Elliot's left arm. This simultaneous action of both hands is practiced in the Mook Jong form at the end of every section. It's very effective.

The two-way action of one hand pulling and the other striking is a difficult combination to keep up with once you have the hang of the shifting, stepping, and Huen-sao. It'll be like being in a fight with multiple opponents.

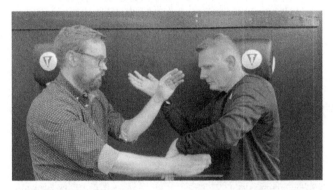

In this sequence I've used the Huen with my left and a Guan-sao with my right to gain this position. I apologize for what looks like repetitive photos but the idea is to be fluid and to be able to change directions as your opponent's energy moves. As always: don't fight force with force while using great force. Go where he isn't; let him help you hit him.

The movement of the hands in this case isn't merely side-to-side as in the momma-poppa roll, but a little back and forth. Combined with the shifting stance, this opens up Elliot's defense.

Again we arrive at the basic strike. It's like a boxer's jab. Sometimes he feints with it, other times he counters. Chi-sao gives you a robust tool box of simple attacks.

In this sequence I'm changing from inside to outside on one line and vice-versa on the other. Again, this is an application of the 3rd section of the Mook Jong.

The opponent is often unable to keep up with positional changes and directional shifts. In this case, Elliot is again open on the inside line. My right hand controls Elliot's left wrist. If you look at videos of Ip Ching rolling, you'll notice that he often uses tactics such as these and doesn't arbitrarily restrict the contact point to the forearms. Much of the usefulness of Chi-sao is lost if we don't "look beyond the pointing finger," so to say.

Notice here the lower position. There's no rule written in the heavens that says Chi-sao can't be practiced from an in-fighter's crouch. A good Wing Chun man/woman should be able to lower their center of gravity to accommodate a wrestler and, therefore, protect their legs from a takedown.

In this photo, though it's hard to follow the action, I've shifted to my right while smoothly redirecting Elliot's energy using the Huen-sao/Guan Sao of the Mook Jong Section Three principles. The change of angles and hand positions opens Elliot's inside line to attack.

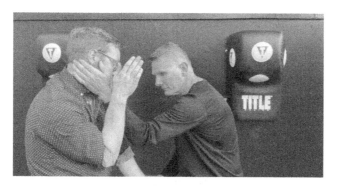

Stepping in, I take advantage of the opening and smack the daylights out of Elliot who went home and cried afterwards. Just kidding.

This is the result of shifting and "running" the hands. See how it opens his defense? If there's tension in your technique it's often a result of not moving/shifting properly. Furthermore, and this is obviously hard to convey in a photo, both my hands were moving in different directions. This is a key component to good Wing Chun: the use of directional variance of the hands applying pressure/dissolving pressure while in movement.

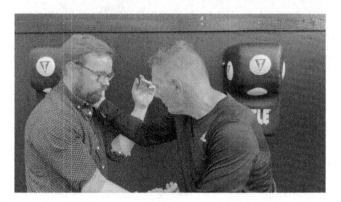

Huen-sao and shifting opens up the basic attack. The more tense the enemy is, and the less skillful he is in defending his center-mass targets (that's everyone in the world basically), the more effective this is.

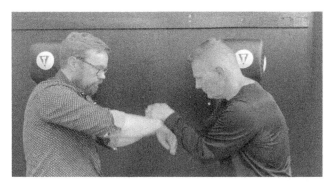

Because of Elliot's pressure on left arm I initiate the circling hand. The better we get at Huen-sao the less we fight force with force and the more we can take advantage of the opponent's tension.

I'm shifting a little to my right to cover the circle-hand action while simultaneously keeping appropriate pressure on the "weak-side" so I don't get clobbered by Elliot's left.

Again we have a basic attack that's not so basic when you consider the factors that made it possible. The attack, as you can see, also came with Seung-ma (forward step) to take advantage of the open angle. The best attacks are combined with footwork so as to totally obliterate the enemy's position. Standing still and playing "gotcha" is a silly bit of business.

Elliot's left arm is exerting pressure on my right, so I initiate a circling hand.

Not being a doofus, he reacts to cut off the Huen-sao on that side. No problem. I shift back and take advantage of his over-correction. You see, the ability to change directions is key. This is why we must train progressively and not rush the process. When I started my right-hand action, he moved quickly to adjust but didn't cover the other side.

This left him open for the left-hand attack.

The action of both hands being independent, along with the shifting of angles, and footwork to absorb or exert force - working altogether at once - is a hard combination to defeat.

A quick follow up. Notice how I'm moving forward and "sucking the air out of the pocket." This prevents him from making adjustments and/or countering. Take his balance as you strike whenever you can.

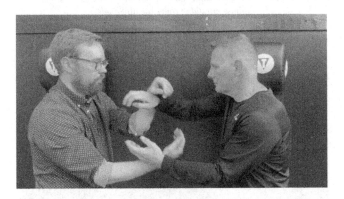

Here we are back in the momma-poppa.

In this case, I begin to shift left. As he adjusts, I shift back the other way to cut him off. The Huen-sao and shifting are working in tandem. Practice the Mook-Jong and Chum Kiu often in order to develop the proper mechanics of shifting or else you'll lose forward pressure.

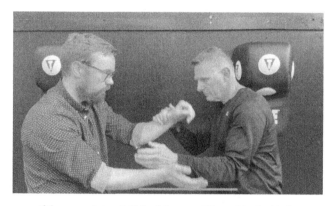

If the enemy is too rigid the follow-up shift combined with the Huen-sao opens him up as you can see. Notice that both my hands have changed position...the left is now on the inside and vice-versa on the right.

And here's the basic attack again, created by Huen-sao and footwork. It's simple, yes, but not easy.

The follow-up is also key. We aren't playing for one-shot kill. In Wing Chun the Faan-sao principle (repeating hand) is imperative to in-fighting success.

More Faan-sao (repeating hand) follow-up. Once you get the guy going, finish him.

This sequence of several hits should happen in a flash. A common mistake in Wing Chun is for novices to fall in love with the speed of the chain punch principle and miss the application principles that make it effective. Here's the idea in action. After gaining control you can "let your hands go." Doing that without first gaining position is foolhardy.

3

THE DRILL

A fair complaint against any fighting system is that it has no pressure testing. This testing, be sure, is essential for the simple human fact that under pressure men don't perform better than they do when calm. How are we to know, therefore, that what we do in the safety and tranquility of our kwoon (school or gym) won't fail us when forced to fight for our lives? This is the question of questions.

That Wing Chun is identified as a close-quarter combat systematic is a given. All things that exist, the laws of logic tell us, are specific things. A thing is the thing it is and not something else. Such is logic's law of identity. The Marines, for example, are not the Navy or Air Force although all of them are branches of the military. Each has a specific function and that function (identity) demands a certain type of training. Sure, there will be similarities but tank commanders and fighter pilots must logically have different training drills.

To this end we say that Wing Chun is more like a combat art than a combat sport. The modern martial artist, if we can say in fact that there is one these days, diluted as the field is, sopped through with the leakage of civilized sport thinking, is closer to a Marine than a boxer. How so? Because the Marine trains for a lethality that's unthinkable to, say, a boxer. Likewise, a martial art such as Wing Chun loses its identity when it omits this foundational fact. Though modern martial art training will rationally resemble the trades of boxing and MMA on some counts, they must logically differ on the critical count. An MMA fighter whose goal is lethality isn't a man one wants to go a few rounds with, right?

When not thinking in principles, which is to eschew wisdom, man has a terrible tendency to swing to extremes. We see it in politics, relationships, work...everywhere. The consequences of a mistake finally get bad enough to draw our attention and then, now alert to our error, we often over-correct. Most excesses in political movements are the result of this. Growing up I saw this with my father's tendency to let our chores slide a bit and then something would set him off and he'd overreact and we were treated to a hard crackdown. Scrubbing, dusting, cleaning, folding...for a while we were in a sort of domestic Marine Corps.

Well, for years up until Bruce Lee, the martial arts community had grown soft. So-called masters who were obese or adorned with the muscle mass of a desktop computer were the norm. And then there was Bruce Lee. And after that there was Royce Gracie and the UFC in 1993. Suddenly the evidence was undeniable. We needed sparring. We needed pressure testing as well as basic fitness.

Amen and amen.

The problem was that, per our usual lack of wisdom, the pendulum swung rather too far the other way. It's the *ex-girl-friend/wife syndrome.* You know...she had problems. Yeah. That's why you broke up. Sure. But the natural reaction is to literally demonize her, which is quite rather a bridge too far. A few years pass - or maybe a few decades - and then we mellow out a little. We realize that, yeah, there were problems, but she wasn't actually Lucifer's spawn.

(Except for my ex-girlfriend. She was Satan's little sister who's still probably plotting the evil overthrow of humanity through which all the world will be cast into darkness and suffering. And she's plotting this unspeakable evil while she's in the bathroom. Why else would she take so long in there? It's all part of her evil plan and I got out just in time. Or maybe I need a few more decades to chill. Whatever.)

Anyway, this is what happened with the whole sparring thing. Now the martial art world is replete with "coaches" rather than instructors who have one simple answer to every combat question: *do you even spar, bro?* Anyone who has ever worked in a large corporation or in government (which is the largest corporation of all) knows what it's like when the whole machine overreacts and has a bee in its bureaucratic bonnet. The focus shifts so much to one side that other things begin to suffer. And that's exactly the case with sparring.

Sparring develops timing. This means, in an almost criminal understatement, that it helps you "see" strikes coming at you. The natural response to a strike coming at your face is never the right one. We either don't react and get clobbered (because we freeze) or overreact (pulling away so that we lose our vision and balance) and get clobbered with the next shot. In short, we either have no timing (can't see anything at all at fighting speed) or we have no *grace under pressure* (as Hemingway aptly put it). Safe sparring is the surest way to correct these two problems. If we can't see things at full speed because our central nervous system isn't used to it, and/or we haven't developed the discipline to react with skill when under fire, our knowledge is simply superfluous. It's like dressing up but staying in the house. It's like buying a great car when you don't know how to drive. Or it's like trying to reason with your mother-in-law.

Anyway.

Sparring also helps develop accuracy - because throwing strikes at someone who's moving and trying to hit you is much harder than hitting a heavy bag.

Like I said, this is almost a criminal understatement of the benefits of good sparring. What it does, though, despite my hasty definition, is alert the good reader to the *identity* of the exercise. Sparring clearly isn't fighting; it's not self-defense. It's an organized drill with an identifiable nature. Thus, it's a means to the end of fixing the problems of bad timing, and lack of accuracy and technical disci-

pline. Remember, everything that is, is a specific thing and not something else in the same way/context. The current obsession with
sparring is, therefore, a hasty generalization or, as Bruce Lee put it
(about boxing) over daring. Why? Because it's leaving out relevant
detail. Yes, we must spar but we must not *only* spar.

The apostles of sparring will quite naturally protest against any
criticism of their irrational belief. I know because I've been there.
Anyone who's followed us on YouTube knows that we have a *boxing*
program as well as *Wing Chun* and *Jeet Kune Do*. I love boxing and
always have. I truly think that everyone should learn to box as a base
discipline (but that's a book for another time). When I was a younger
man - and more competitive - I too conflated sparring with self-
defense and thus was guilty of the irrationality infecting so many of
my martial brethren. I too thought that if people weren't going at it in
sparring then they were no better than that spawn of Satan ex of
mine. Maybe just not as completely evil as she was. (And for the
record, to be clear: I never actually dated anyone so morally
heinous...oh, and my mother-in-law is quite a sweetie...I just like the
jokes). Sifu Lamar Davis, that great apostle of Original JKD, once
chided me for turning my JKD class into a boxing program via too
much sparring. He had a point. I was too stubborn to admit that then
(give me a break...I very young, a veritable toddler in my mid-20's,
and wasn't as extraordinarily wise as I am now...nor as humble...just
saying). The lesson is clear: if you're gonna admit to a mistake, be
funny about it.

So, seriously, the key to resolving the issue is in understanding
the law of identity. Sparring helps with those specific things like
timing and accuracy and grace under pressure. Those qualities are
essential, yes. But, that said, sparring isn't and can't be actual self-
defense due to a myriad of tactical, legal, moral, and, of course, safety
issues. But the premise of it is application. That's the key. What
we're really saying when we fall into the "do you spar, bro" philosophy is that one's estimation of reality is not the same thing as reality.

Bingo!

Exactly!

That's the crux of the issue.

The reality of a non-cooperative opponent really trying to hurt you is vastly different than shadow boxing or bag work, right? The thing the sparring bro is really saying is that objective reality is the governor, not my feelings, hopes or dreams. He's making a philosophical declaration about the nature of reality. The problem is, he's dealing with philosophy but doesn't know it. He's a *hard pragmatist* who's saying that unless he sees it with his own eyes it doesn't count. Pragmatism, the late R.C. Sproul once said, as a test of truth is great; as a theory of truth, however, it's a disaster. The conditions of the test may or may not be repeatable. That's the foundational contradiction of the sparring bro. He's assuming what is demonstrably false, which is that the conditions of the "test" are and always will be identical or near enough to the reality of what he's talking about - that being self-defense. That's a dangerously irrational assumption.

He's right about the need to test and prepare but wrong about the conclusions drawn from those tests. He's right that reality is the final arbiter and then wrong because he then insists that he's put reality in a bottle - or, in this case, a cage or ring. He's right that one must be brought to test the applications of *their* personal ability to apply techniques and tactics in a non-cooperative environment, yet erroneous when he thinks that the nature of non-cooperation will always be identical.

The major areas of contradiction are clear. Sparring is voluntary; violence is not. Sparring involves safety equipment, sure footing, safe borders like ropes or a cage, a single opponent, and restriction of targets. Fighting in self-defense will absolutely have none of these characteristics. Thus, we can assume that the logical student, the one who takes reality seriously, sees the critical impact of those issues and seeks a rational means of preparing for them.

Without safety equipment we must conclude that certain types of striking may very well injure us. More still, without gloves, headgear and shin guards, our defensive movements must be adjusted. A defensive structure that relies on things that won't be present in real violence is to be avoided.

Bad footing must be considered. Clutter and hard objects serve as serious dangers to the self-defender. A safe environment to spar/train in is an absolute moral and legal must. Yet this seriously distorts the reality of self-defense. Windows, curbs, cars, other people, counters, stairs, etc...one's combat systematic isn't logical if it doesn't prepare for these potentialities.

Borders. Yes, this is seriously overlooked too. One can't "lean on the ropes" or "use the cage" on a hiking trail, a stairwell, or in a mob attack. The "border" may very well be a lake, a cliff, or a window.

And what about multiple opponents? A classic mistake is to get sucker-punched by an opportunistic knucklehead because your training was hyper-focused on only one opponent.

And finally, though this isn't an exhaustive list, soft targets simply must be accounted for in a logical combat systematic.

In all, sparring is a critical component of one's self-defense training insofar as we need to understand timing and accuracy under aggressive pressure. Nevertheless, it isn't, nor can it be, the reality of self-defense. Only self-defense is the reality of self-defense. All the training is, speaking logically - training and not the thing itself. An attempt to make our training/sparring the real thing - that is, to add such variables as these - is to leave the realm of reason. It throws off the necessary bridle of sanity and safety and makes us a one-hit YouTube or TikTok wonder (because we all love to watch people be dangerously stupid). Any alleged coach/teacher who tries to fly too close to the sun isn't a leader; they're a sociopath masquerading as a martial artist.

So, how do we account for those other things? Well, to put it bluntly, "do you even Chi-Sao, bro?"

Indeed, Chi-sao is the only drill this writer is aware of that checks these boxes and allows us to train for these variables *safely*. And, yes, safety is the absolute critical component. A martial art system that eschews one's well-being is like a marriage where one spouse is cheating all the time. It's a contradiction in terms. Crippling oneself in the pursuit of personal safety is the stupidest idea since I tried to actually use tools to fix something (there may or may not have been a

National Guard incident, police reports, the weeping of children, some gnashing of teeth, and a hefty repair bill).

Anyway, we pause to note the BIG thing that Chi-sao does that every other training drill either flat out ignores or has no idea how to train dynamically. And dynamic drilling is, like sparring, important because we have to bridge the gap between technique and application. What isn't tested under varying degrees of pressure, after all, can hardly be relied upon in the event of supreme pressure - and that being a violent encounter with an enemy trying to kill you. Boxing doesn't do it. Wrestling doesn't do it. MMA, Muay Thai, kickboxing... nothing gives us a laboratory to develop, test, and refine the tactical/technical foundation of all-out fighting[1].

And, we must solemnly declare, not bombastically, and not by way of truculence, but by way of sober judgment - that absent this we're playing at a violent game, not honest to goodness fighting. Oh, indeed...we men love competition. We love to test ourselves. But actual survival warfare and competition are not the same thing and the closer they become to one another the less intellect is involved. *Hunger Games* or *Running Man* are not viable means of morally consistent entertainment. It took the Christian church a couple of centuries to reform the Roman culture so that they realized, warped and morally ill as they were, that gladiatorial games weren't okay.

And to reiterate, we are in no way advocating, nor would we ever, for the combining of war arts with sporting combat. The desire to see men (or women) die or be maimed for our entertainment is morally repugnant in the extreme. If the U.S. Marine Corps can field an effective killing force without using lethal force in training, then we assume that self-defenders can follow suit.

So, again, the Chi-sao drill is the go-between, the missing ingredient, and the linchpin for effective close-quarter fighting. It alone provides trainees with the non-contradictory platform to test and develop combat reflexes designed to do combat's most essential thing.

The attack and defense of the body's weak targets.

The close-quarter game is one where the neck, throat, jaw, eyes and head are all preeminent targets for the self-defender. A rationally consistent fighting method must both attack and defend these things since they serve as the nerve center of human health. A man with an injured windpipe or eye isn't a well man; his ability to do damage to another person has been greatly diminished if not wholly eradicated.

The omission of this for self-defense is unthinkable. No self-defense system is logical if it doesn't account for vital targets in cluttered environment at close-range. If for no other reason Wing Chun is a logical science of self-defense if this is understood properly and then appropriately trained, which is to say systematically. The Chi-sao drill is, therefore, truly the genius of Wing Chun. We certainly agree with that except we'd like to add that it's not merely this but the genius of *all close-range self-defense systematics*. If one has never sparred it's safe to say that they will not have the critical attributes of timing and accuracy. Likewise, if a man or woman doesn't know Chi-sao (properly), then he/she doesn't have logical close-range self-defense skill.

Like sparring, Chi-sao has a very diversified use.

One can spar at varying levels of intensity, right? Not only that but elements of tools are also to be considered. Are we just boxing or kickboxing? Are we using takedowns? Any blows from the ground? You see? Sparring always presumes a set of standards in order to assure the growth of skill and the all-important safety of the participants. It's the same with Chi-sao.

For example, with the goal of Chi-sao in mind - that is, developing non-contradictory fighting skill at close range - a teacher will have a student engage in basic "rolling hands" (*poon-sao*). This is the lightest of light sparring that a newbie would do with a coach in the boxing ring. Poon-sao develops the coordination to use both hands in the primary inside/outside contact positions of taan/bong and fook-sao. This phase will take as long as it takes. It's dependent upon the student. The goal is to use the techniques of Siu Lim Tao with a partner while in a predetermined contact position.

A newbie in sparring is going to be making all sorts of mistakes. He's going to drop his guard, he's going to lean forward when trying to land a punch - thereby exposing his chin, and so on. This is why no professional coach would ever allow a guy to go hard until he's had enough light sparring experience to reasonably address these issues. Nevertheless, as all boxing coaches know, these mistakes, as elemental as they are, never go completely away. The basics are always the thing. It's the same with Chi-sao. Our goal is to control the enemy, close off access to our targets and attack the enemy all at once. Doing this consistently - and at full speed/power while under pressure - is the key. Such is the purpose of our training.

Well, like sparring, Chi-sao will continually increase in pressure and complexity (that is, in the number of variables involved). After a student has gained proficiency in the basics of rolling hands, he/she learns basic strikes. Then they learn basic defenses against those strikes. Then they learn to counter-attack and follow-up. Footwork, shifting, more speed and pressure are then added. Pushing and pulling is added. And in this process minor drills can be used to supplement the main drill. Doing *Paak-sao* drill, or the *Lop-sao* drill... all cross-hand practice is a derivative of the grandfather of close-range drills, Chi-sao.

4

OVERCOMING TENSION

L et's face a serious truth. It's the elephant in the room and we really need to talk about it. For reasons we'll get to in a little bit, people in Wing Chun avoid it. We won't. We must address it.

What is it? Tension.

It's an enormous mistake to train Chi-sao without addressing the subject of overcoming tension because that's exactly what we're gonna see in a real fight. There are, after all, three types of physical "energy" insofar as bridge contact is concerned. Pressing, yielding, and static. It's a colossal blunder to force students to train only with and against yielding pressure when in reality we're guaranteed to encounter the other two. Of course, the correct approach utilizes soft or yielding energy to defeat pressing and static tension, this can only be achieved by training against them.

A thing to consider is that proper Wing Chun should make us stronger and faster than our enemy on the inside. The springy power that comes from good structure trained well should be devastating to an untrained aggressor. If all this Wing Chun training doesn't provide us superiority in these critical areas then it's useless. Actually, worse than useless because false security is dangerous. A man that knows he's not good at something is in far less danger than one who erroneously believes he is. False knowledge is the root of all sorts of hell on earth. Remember those poor saps on the old TV show *American Idol* who thought they could sing? How many young lads think boxing will be easy and then go and get bopped in the honker? How many catastrophic wars have started with the lunacy of "this won't take long at all" being chanted all the way to the bloody trenches?

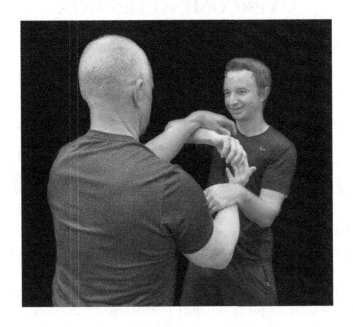

So, the thing is, the enemy isn't going to attack with "soft" force. No. He's coming at us hard and fast and if we don't finish him with strikes and there's a tie-up (a bridge), we're going to experience serious pressure. Good Chi-sao training must take this into account by progressively training students to use springy structure. This can't be done by literally omitting pressure and insisting that students use only "good form" - which is to say, springy force. For crying out loud, the whole idea of using the springy force is so that we can actually fight the heavy, driving pressure of the enemy in the first place.

Jeez.

So, why do we do that? Why are most Wing Chun students forbidden from training against/with the actual type of force that's realistic?

Here are the top excuses/reasons.

First, teachers have stopped keeping the main thing the main thing. They've forgotten that Wing Chun is a "war-art". They've lost the plain truth. It's the forest and trees thing. Everything in a war-art comes back to the primary purpose, which is not getting killed in a fight. Simple. This just seems too crude and barbaric for people who like to think of themselves as civilized.

Second, traditionalists misconstrue, due to the previous misconception, the facts of training. A student must learn good structure before learning to handle and apply overwhelming force. Reversing this order leads to chaos. That said, not moving past the early emphasis on relaxation and good form leads to impotence. The relaxation and structure are there in order to maximize the use of force. That's the key. If a student is too stiff and/or has poor form then they can't move on and apply the type of scientific pressure we're talking about.

The "traditional" approach (it's better, perhaps, to call it "highly formalized training") is valid only if it insists upon the correct apprehension and repetition of the fundamentals so that the student develops the neuromuscular reflexes needed for infighting. Again, the goal of the training is the key thing and the Wing Chun fighter should be able to simply overwhelm other fighters at close-range. They should have functional power and speed that dominate the enemy. Why? Because other systems eschew the fundamentals of war-art infighting. What we see, though, is that many have turned Chi-sao into a game of fancy slapping or hyper-technical nonsense in which arbitrary rules are placed on the drill that literally emasculate it.

Third, the instructor doesn't want students to touch him.

Ah...imagine that at a boxing gym. Imagine you have a student who is training diligently several days a week and yet still can't even land a shot on the seniors or head coach. That's preposterous. It's a sign that the goal of the training drills is flawed. Of course, an advanced student is going to be better than a junior practitioner, but the simplicity of Chi-sao, like boxing, means that some contact should be made. Once the student has the fundamentals down they should be engaging in heavy drills with the seniors and/or instructor. They should be learning to "win" insofar as the drills go. That is, they should be developing and *honing the habits of infighting dominance*.

But this takes an instructor who has both mastered the craft himself and desires that the students get as good, if not better, than he/she is. This is a serious problem in many martial art schools. The students are never truly taught how to get as good or better than the teacher. In boxing the emphasis of the coach is on making a winner out of the pupil. Think of Cus D'Amato and Mike Tyson. The basics done very, very well - and very fast and hard too - should be the emphasis.

With this said, the idea should be clear. We learn the forms and perform the drills early in our training so that we develop the correct muscle memory to apply the Wing Chun theory and structures in fighting. The first order is, therefore, to *develop the weapon*. But since fighting is going to be an intense clash of speed and strength, good Chi-sao progressively trains up the student to both receive and deliver extreme levels of pressure. At first, all students will respond to incoming pressure with tension - both of body and mind. Chi-sao is, in our thinking, the primary way of developing a coordinated and logical response to this reality.

The Muay Thai clinch and/or wrestling are excellent "types" through which we can understand the nature of Chi-sao training. Poor teachers try and make mysteries out of this. There shouldn't be any. Good practice should be making us more efficient, via technical skill under varying degrees of pressure, at achieving our primary goals. To this end, we need both enough real-world pressure and common-sense realism - and this must be done safely - especially considering the targets involved.

This is the edge that something like Muay Thai or a grappling art will often have over Wing Chun if we aren't careful. Because they're using training equipment and safety rules (and target restrictions), they can use higher levels of aggression/resistance in their drills. In Wing Chun we're attacking vulnerable targets, which we can't do in any form of realistic sparring. This is where Chi-sao must come in. Rightly used, it's a specialized grappling drill for strikers and a striking drill for grapplers. It's not wholly different from wrestling but a more scientific version of it.

If we use this as our interpretive principle then we no longer see Chi sao as a drill that's set apart from the rest of fighting. The tactical tension between what we know to be true about infighting from methods like boxing, Muay Thai, and wrestling and Chi-sao disappears. Indeed, we know that we don't fight like we're doing Siu Lim Tao...we fight with the structures and principles of the form. We fight *from* the form but aren't bound by it. Well, it's the same thing with Chi-sao! We shouldn't be trying to in-fight as though we're doing Chi-sao. Liberation from this error alone will radically alter one's Wing Chun.

Moreover, it saves us from the twin philosophical errors of hyper-traditionalism and anarchy. The technical skill of Chi-sao is there to assist us in getting the job done in a non-contradictory manner. A pure wrestler whose muscle memory literally exposes his most vulnerable targets will run into the shredder of good Wing Chun *if*, in fact, the Wing Chun fighter applies the principles and structures of Chi-sao without being bound by them.

If, however, the Wing Chun fighter has been led to believe that lowering his center of gravity is some kind of sin, he'll never get the chance to attack. He'll be slammed to the ground in short order. Just as bad, if he's only done *"love-sao"* all soft and tender because he's been told that using force is crude "external Wing Chun" then he'll get blown out of there. (There's an opposite to the "love-sao" error too. If we're overly concerned with using power rather than technical structure and springy energy, we turn Chi-sao into a veritable tug-of-war. Light Chi-sao, where the participants agree to work on fluidity in order to overcome *their own emotional and muscular tension,* is absolutely part of a logical curriculum just like light sparring drills are in boxing.)

You see, the key is in not going to extremes. We should start with the structure of chi-sao and learn that structure so well that we can seamlessly adjust to any type of infighter.

5

SIMULTANEOUS ATTACK & DEFENSE - LIN SIU DAAI DA

The best defense is a good offense.

Check.

But what exactly is a good offense? It's certainly not foolish aggression. It can't be that any more than running at a machine gun nest is a good plan. You know...it's kind of hard to run faster than bullets.

There's a thin but important line of demarcation between being aggressive and being stupid and wisdom calls for us to mark it clearly. That's what we're trying to do in Chi-sao. We're being taught and trained to be highly aggressive without compromising our defense; we're developing combat reflexes to shut down our enemy's attack while simultaneously setting up our own. It's not either-or; it's offensive-defense...defensive-offense.

The novelist/philosopher Ayn Rand once remarked that in any compromise between food and poison, poison wins. What she meant was that certain ideas and ideologies were poison and couldn't be safely mixed with others. She was a rabid anti-commie, having escaped Soviet Russia and come to America after her college years. Whatever one likes to think about her philosophy of *Objectivism*[1], it's very hard to argue with her insistence that Marxism is an evil philosophy incompatible with political liberty and individual rights.

Likewise, when thinking about offensive-defense and the practice of Chi-sao, we need to keep in mind that there are some things that are bad ideas. And because of the stakes being life or death, safety or severe injury, we should be vigilant. We should be circumspect and rigorous in regard to our self-defense so as to avoid being on the wrong side of that line.

ONE WAY of seeing this is that Chi-sao provides a close-range "fighting measure." A fighting measure is the safe distance we keep in which the enemy must step in to attack. In other words, the *measure* is to fighting what the no tailgating rule is to driving. Reaction time is the reality no one can escape. If the enemy is too close, then our ability to react to his initiation is diminished and we'll likely be hit. Several factors impact one's *practice* of the measure, especially reach and speed of the enemy. The faster the enemy, the more space is needed to react to his attack. It's a simple matter of physics.

There are also several intelligent strategies to help one's reaction time. For example, movement is a key. It's simply harder to reach a moving target than one that's predictable. Second, a self-defender might use a barrier that forces the attacker to maneuver around, such as a table or chair. Also, there's contact...and this is where Chi-sao comes in.

You see, a grappler ties up a guy "on the inside" so as to negate the physical reality of reaction time. By controlling the other guy at close range - clinching with him - you can bypass the reflex lag that exists without contact. All grapplers live and breathe on this point. Being at close range without physical contact with the enemy is a recipe for a KO. The hard rule is, at close range - that is, within the fighting measure distance - lack of contact-control leaves a fighter exposed because there's no time to react.

It's for this reason that Chi-sao is a *grappling drill* because it stands upon the truth that inside the reflex lag line there must be contact.

But, of course, Wing Chun isn't a contradictory fighting science of self-defense so, as we must continually remind ourselves, it accounts for combat variables left out of purely sporting environments. If Chi-sao is looked at properly in this light we keep the "poison" out of it. In another way of saying it, Wing Chun's Chi-sao is *combat grappling* in that it's practice in the range of fighting where the reflex lag challenge is at its most extreme. If Chi-sao doesn't include and adapt to this point then it's worse than useless...in fact, it's dangerous...it's a form of combat malpractice.

We repeat: at close-range, within the fighting measure line where the defender has no time to react, it's suicidal to not control the balance and striking ability of the enemy. Thus, the first thing to know about Chi-sao is that the arm positions taught in the drill are *types* of a close-range fighting measure. The idea of a good offense being the best defense can't mean that the offense forsakes defense. What good does it do for an army to go on the attack and then return home to find that they don't have one anymore? Chi-sao, therefore, teaches first the type of hand positions that are optimal for infighting efficiency.

Fook-sao, Taan-Sao, and *Bong-Sao* are the physical structures that, once mastered and integrated into one's neuro-muscular system, provide the trainee with both the technical and tactical means of scientific infighting. Without them, or by doing them in error, the trainee loses the ability to integrate Wing Chun's close-range/contact systematic. He may hit but he gets hit; he plays one element of the system over against another. Unless we master the structures within the drill we lose the very heart of the system.

Simultaneous attack and defense. This is the heart of Wing Chun.

The Wing Chun fighter must observe the fighting measure when not in contact-control with the enemy. This tactical misunderstanding has caused lots of grief, not just for Wing Chun students, but for everyone. It's the *chiu-ying/bi-ying* principle applied. If the enemy can face you (that is, if he's set and ready) he shouldn't be able to reach you. And if he's able to reach you, he shouldn't be able to face you. That's smart fighting right there in a nutshell. To best understand this, reverse the order and see what happens.

If the enemy is set and mobilized in front of you (chiu-ying), go ahead and stand right there and wait to see what happens. Such fighting "inside the pocket" without a positional advantage is fool-hardy in the extreme. If the enemy is determined, and strong enough to hurt you, you're in big trouble.

Furthermore, and this is a common mistake (dreadfully common) in Wing Chun these days, poor understanding of Chi-sao leads us to get contact with the enemy but not control his balance. In this case the enemy still has chiu-ying in principle because, even if not exactly facing, he has the ability to attack with power. Remember, the chiu-ying principle is a robust one that subsumes a good bit of tactical/technical detail. If the enemy has contact with you *and* has his balance, then you don't have control and shouldn't be there.

We should say it again: if the opponent has his balance when you're in contact range, close enough to be hit without him having to close the gap, then we're in serious jeopardy.

The fighting measure principle rests upon the fact of reflex lag. So, to understand and apply simultaneous attack and defense we must correctly apply the principle of negation that the measure rests upon. Use of the fighting measure at long range, and the fook-taan-bong systematic when in contact, are the applications, technically and tactically, of the lin siu daai da (simultaneous attack and defense) principle. We often hear about how Wing Chun is a system of concepts, not techniques but fail to logically define what this means. Here it is. Vagueness is the scourge of life. Vacillation is not a moral virtue. Wing Chun is a system of simultaneous attack and defense and, therefore, Chi-sao is the system's primary drill to achieve this goal from within the fighting measure. Both parties *agree* to work within its structural framework so that *both parties learn the technical applications of the lin siu daai da concept.* Failure to properly understand this reality, and the drill's relationship (as an integrative aspect, or bridge, from the theory to the practice) to application creates contradiction within the systematic and incoherence with the facts of reality.

A grappler ties a guy up and "smothers" his ability to strike. He does this by both positional and balance control. He doesn't need total domination right away. Initially, he needs negation...he needs to get into position without getting KO'd or taken down. The principle is the same for Wing Chun fighters. Again, we repeat: the principle is precisely the same and that's the correct way to understand and practice Chi-sao. Ignorance of this reality is why our Chi-sao practice and skill isn't translating into fighting success. The thought that Chi-sao exists as a thing unto itself, some high form of martial mystery, has clouded our thinking and made us do very foolish things. Sure, it's flashy and cool and we can get hooked on that.

That's called infatuation, by the way.

And a man or woman is never thinking clearly when they're infatuated. And such passion is hardly ever logical, right? I mean, no one should get married merely on the basis of a crush but that's sort of what happens with Chi-sao. We jettison the obvious. And it's obvious that on the inside we absolutely must simultaneously control the enemy's balance and striking ability. We must "smother" his attack capacity through scientific structure and positioning. If we don't control his balance and/or limbs, he's free to attack at extremely close-range where the reflex lag will treat us like gravity does if we step off a cliff. If we ignore this we end up building an elaborate sand castle of a drill. But such Wing Chun training is all low tide stuff. Then, when the Wing Chun fighter who'd been lying to himself about in-fighting reality and Chi-sao ends up flat on his back because of a double-leg, or KO'd by an overhand or hook, he looks like a child crying on the beach when the tide ruins his masterpiece.

So, yeah, the first order of business to understand is the "inside measure" component of Chi-sao. Though have to learn the arm/hand positions in order to gain correct muscle memory, we mustn't lose the big picture. Once this is done, the student learns how to use structural pressure and positional control to take away the balance of the enemy. And these need to happen simultaneously. Thus, "advanced" Chi-sao is a literal pressure test. It has to combine the primary hand structures of the system with non-contradictory striking, pushing and pulling. Any Chi-sao training that doesn't do this is unrealistic. It's set-up for disaster...like going to see your ex for help with your self-esteem.

Just as a grappler's clinch intends to prohibit your striking him, the Wing Chun fighter's "bridging" should accomplish the same thing. The difference is that this isn't done in a manner that contradicts the rest of the structure and tactical goal of all-out fighting. It's not, repeat not, an either-or proposition. A good Wing Chun man/woman intends and trains to apply simultaneous attack and defense on the inside.

And Chi-sao is the primary way of training to achieve this goal.

We need to pause for a moment. We need to slow down and remember the exigent point that Chi-sao is a drill and not actual fighting. It's a prescription, not health itself. The technical manner in which we learn to train for these things must not be confused with the thing itself. In other words, taan-sao, fook-sao, and bong sao are not infighting. They're types of contact points. They aren't nouns. They're verbs. A good taan-sao is almost, therefore, a contradiction in terms insofar as fighting is concerned because a "palm-up hand" is a description of something and a "spreading hand" is reference to directional force. The same goes with all other Wing Chun techniques and if we're going to gain skill in self-defense we've gotta get past this sticking point (bad pun...sorry).

The drill itself is a necessary evil in that we must have a means of training at clinch/contact range. Acknowledgment of all the aforementioned stuff doesn't translate into action unless we've honed the correct structural detail into living reflex against varying degrees of force/pressure. Boxing and other striking disciplines can give us good distance control, timing and accuracy. But how do we achieve the goals of infighting (as far as self-defense is concerned)? BJJ and wrestling won't teach us to achieve those objectives but you can understand why many people flock to those disciplines. They reason well only up to the point of combat realism and then break down. Wing Chun trainees should understand that Chi-sao is the logical answer that bridges the gap between "pure" striking and grappling - or, more to the point, pure sport combat.

An effective and non-contradictory inside fighting method must "smother" the enemy's ability to strike and effectively grapple. If Wing Chun can't do this, why bother with it since striking and grappling obviously work? Chi-sao is, therefore, Wing Chun's primary training drill to achieve this objective. This will be dynamic, of course, and require adjustments in real time. It must neutralize and/or control the enemy's balance. It can't allow for too much free movement on the part of the enemy lest he get free to strike...and at such close range this could be catastrophic. More still, it must not leave the self-defender vulnerable for a takedown either. In all, the "bridge" or clinch of the rational infighter neutralizes the enemy's ability to either strike or grapple effectively. Wing Chun's Chi-sao, rightly understood and practiced, is the only dynamic training drill that safely and logically achieves these objectives.

On top of this the infighter seeks to use bridging technique that controls the enemy while not canceling out attacks on the enemy's thermal exhaust ports. The structure trained through Wing Chun should allow the rational infighter the ability to achieve the previously described defensive objectives while also setting up attack to the enemy's weakest targets. And all of this should be simultaneous. This isn't to say that it happens all at once in application, but in essence. The enemy will have something to say about how quickly the Wing Chun infighter achieves this goal. The saying of "let him help you hit him" comes to mind. Everyone is going to leave something open at some point. The nature of aggression is such that the defender, so long as they adhere to the principles and structural heart of what they've trained to do, will have a target to fire at before long. It might take several seconds, or it might happen right away. That's up to the enemy.

In the interim, though, the Wing Chun infighter must be able to maintain the primary objectives - especially the action of shutting down the enemy's ability to function with offensive effectiveness - while seeking attack opportunities of their own. Also, and importantly, if the defensive aspect of the structure is compromised, the Wing Chun fighter should be able to disengage for safety (it's not a sin, if one loses control on the inside, to step off-line and/or back to a safe distance). Taking their balance doesn't mean losing one's own. And control is the central thing. Always.

IN THIS WAY, THE FIRST "PHASE" of Chi-sao training teaches the student how to both attack and defend the central command unit. By that we mean the head, jaw, neck and throat. Any damage to these areas greatly diminishes a fighter's functional capacity. Therefore, the basic hand positions of Chi-sao are taught so that the student learns the most effective means of attacking and defending these areas. There's no scientific training method that achieves both of these goals like Wing Chun. Most other systematics altogether ignore strikes to the jaw, throat, neck and eyes – offensively as well as defensively. Others that train them don't have consistent and safe means of pressure testing them so they end up relying solely upon overwhelming force and have no training provisions for overcoming obstacles and problem solving like Chi-sao does. This is Wing Chun's primary advantage over other combat methodologies[2].

The second phase, speaking broadly, teaches the student to add footwork and pressure. At first this should be done smoothly and with only as much pressure needed so as to preserve good technique and develop sound muscle memory. As the student matures, more pressure should be added until such a point where the student is literally able to go "all-out" with minimal or zero loss of relaxed springiness, mechanical skill and, of course, safety to the trainees.

Locking, breaking, throwing, short kicks, knees, elbows...every tool and tactic is on the table. After the student has mastered the aforementioned, they should be "playing" with all these. Rigid adherence to the basic chi-sao structure by advanced students is like a dude using training wheels in the Tour-de-France. The goal is simultaneous attack and defense, not rigid adherence to the structures *although it's those structures that provide it.* Thus, Wing Chun is an integrated systematic that has no internal contradictions and is consistent with the nature of hand-to-hand violence.

6

THERMAL EXHAUST PORT

Star Wars fans will instantly get the reference of the chapter's title. We're talking about a single shot that can blow up the enemy Death Star. Well, to show that God loves us and wants us to be happy, He designed the world in which the biggest and baddest among us can be brought down with such well-placed strikes. The systematic logic of Wing Chun is such that it doesn't suppress the obvious. Each of us are walking around, no matter what our bench press is, no matter how amazing our deadlift, with *multiple* thermal exhaust ports.

Eyes, jaw, throat, neck, and certainly the groin.

A sufficient strike to any of these targets is going to greatly diminish an enemy if not outright finish him.

Oh, and let's not forget about the knees and ankles. Those aren't exactly built to take damage either, you know. And if you're wearing a good set of shoes...ah, the damage is quite a thing. No, let's not forget about that at all. Most people do. It's selective awareness. It's wishful thinking. A dude walking around in work-boots has a set of brass-knuckles for his feet and from a clinch/tie-up, his close-range kicking is a nightmare.

If the enemy leaves the middle open this is what could/should happen. Chi-sao training prepares us to reflexively spring forward and attack the central-control systems of the enemy. The brutality of such tactics is exactly why true martial artists must be men/women of the utmost self-control and respect. We aren't going to get into "fender-bender" confrontations because we know how brutal combat truly is.

A uniquely human characteristic is our capacity to suppress the obvious. We go into debt. We overeat. We leave the house late and then fume that traffic is bad. We go out with the person we know is a little dodgy in the head because they're easy on the eyes. (I've never done those things. I'm just saying that lesser men surely do. Just saying). And, to our point at hand, we develop hand-to-hand fighting systematics that altogether ignore the fact that one quick shot to our jingle bells or eye will drop us faster than Thanos could KO pre-Captain America Steve Rogers. (I know...I know...sorry...Marvel and Star Wars references in the same chapter. I'll try and stay focused.).

Fighting is nasty business. I shouldn't have to say that but, again, there's that suppression of the obvious thing going on. I've learned a valuable lesson in life: if you think that it goes without saying, say it anyway. So, yeah, self-defense is a rough bit of business and if you have trouble with eye-gouging, groin strikes, and dislocated knees, you shouldn't be reading this. You should probably stop kidding yourself and go catch the latest Hallmark movie. Or read a Nicolas

Sparks book. (By way of full confession, I'm married and I've sat through my share of Hallmark films...especially the Christmas ones. If you're single, don't judge me, just snicker and move on, please).

So, anyway, the thing is that we're all walking Death Stars except that we aren't nearly as destructive and we have, in truth, a plethora of thermal exhaust ports. Yeah, we're like badly built Death Stars. The idea of Wing Chun is to systematically train to do the things a lot of people say they'd do in a real fight. People talk about foul tactics but never get around to practicing them. Just the same, the fighters that practice are busy doing lots of sport-dominated methods that prohibit thermal exhaust port attacks. Therefore, their muscle memory is all wonky when it comes to dirty fighting.

This brings us to the obvious question of why these attacks aren't more common if such attacks are so effective? I'll provide the top three reasons I've seen in my years of experience...and yes, that's years...as in I'm getting rather old now...as in, I often make 70's and 80's references in class and people look at me blankly.

The first is that we're talking about combat reflexes that must be developed under pressure. The thing to avoid is the mentality of the perfunctory college student asking, "is this gonna be on the test?" It's gross oversimplification to say, "oh, just hit him in the nether regions" and leave it at that. That's like watching Steph Curry hit 3's and thinking it's easy. And even if you can shoot a three pretty well on your own, things get terribly complicated during a game. Doing it by yourself is one thing. Doing it when someone is trying to stop you is another one entirely.

To do any action well, under pressure, requires technique that can be relied upon and executed when it counts. It also demands a tactical-technical integration...in other words, a systematic.

A few years back a security group came to train with me and the head honcho asked if I could just show his guys "the stuff" without bothering with the forms and Chi-sao. They didn't have time for all that, he said. I understand. People are busy and jobs are demanding. The kids need to get driven all over creation, the dog needs to be fed, emails answered, the lawn mowed and, if you live in Buffalo, you have to shovel through eight feet of snow. In June.

Anyway, I explained that there's a system to everything and Wing Chun was already, when you think about it, stripped to its essentials (or should be anyway). To leave out the relevant training drills and technical development (forms) was, at least in this writer's opinion, intellectually inconsistent.

And I hate that.

So, to get it done right we must have a system in place. Everything in life is about habits because actions have consequences and there's no such thing as a free lunch. Everything requires a price be paid and the price we pay for close-quarter fighting skill and soft-target attacks is disciplined training. If we skip that then we're left with something much less than what we could call a skill[1]. It's more like wishful thinking. Going back to our Steph Curry analogy, you'll notice that sometimes he doesn't shoot the three. Sometimes he drives to the basket. Other times he passes to Klay. Sometimes he passes to Jason Korol and then he drives to the lane, blows by Lebron, jumps over A.D. and slams! (Er...sorry...I was dreaming again. Never mind that.) Back to the point, Steph is a *skillful* basketball player who is great at 3's. Likewise, Wing Chun is a systematic that gives us the key to being a skillful infighter not just a dude who tries to poke people in the eye. Every skill looks easy but we like to say at our Academy that it's simple, not easy. Simple things done under pressure, especially violent pressure, is the hallmark of an abundance of training. Forget this, or try and take a short cut, and you might end up in a very bad way.

Second, and picking up on that last point, some people come looking at it as a short-cut of sorts. Not in the previous way but in the manner of not wanting to train hard. This is a very important thing to understand.

If someone hands you a Glock, you might be a weakling with the muscle mass of your average meatball sandwich, but if you pull that bang switch something lethal is gonna come out of the barrel (assuming you had one in the chamber). You see, if you have a Glock in your hand, you're holding a weapon fashioned by the skill of others. Someone took the time, energy, focus and dedication to manufacture that weapon. It's functional precisely because of all that hard work.

A firearm that's missing a firing pin isn't going to work. It must be fully functional or else the bullet isn't going to fire and do what it's intended to do, right? This is the source of lots of misconceptions about MMA and all that. The guys/gals that compete in the cage are all very strong athletes. That alone, plus their singular determination, makes them formidable. Such a highly conditioned athlete, even if, for the sake of argument, he had technique comparable to a five-year-old throwing a fit, is dangerous. All that strength and speed create problems for the target of their aggression. It's like someone with bad aim shooting at you.

The advantage that a boxer or MMA guy has over many self-defenders is that the former takes physical conditioning seriously and the latter often look for shortcuts. That's a bad idea on many levels but especially here.

So, no, we aren't suggesting that the Wing Chun fighter have the conditioning level of an 80-year-old with a walker and oxygen tank. The Glock fires the bullet. Likewise, *you* must be conditioned enough to fire your weapons as well. If I take a bullet from a magazine and throw it at you, I'm a jerk. To be a murderer I need the acceleration generated by the firearm. The critical difference between a thrown rock and a bullet is the acceleration. It's the same thing with the human body. We need to avoid the mistaken belief that because we're attacking soft targets we can be soft. On the contrary, we must be weapons too...just like the Glock.

Some of us are going to have more physical advantages than others. Nevertheless, everyone needs to develop and increase their basic requirements as Bruce Lee used to call them. All martial artists should be training to get stronger, faster, more endurance and better range of motion. All of that is in service of functional performance as well as general health. An unhealthy martial artist is a contradiction in terms. That said, the goal isn't to be the strongest and fastest, but strong and fast enough. Think about it: it doesn't matter much if I get shot in the head by a 9mm, a .45, a .223, or an artillery shell. I'm dead either way. *How* dead I am is irrelevant to me because I'm dead. I'm not more or less dead, I'm just dead. It's like that here. Combat is a clash of speed and power, so all of us should be training to get enough of those qualities to be functional. After all, there's no way to hurt someone *softly and slowly*.

THIRD, there's improper commitment to taking out the enemy. People are half-hearted. They live in some kind of martial land of gnosticism where they don't want to get their hands dirty. They think real mastery is devoid of emotional ferocity. In the worst cases they disguise cowardice behind the facade of *nice*. They're embarrassed by actual aggression and think all anger is bad. But this is all vanity and smoke. Real self-defense requires indignation - that is, righteous anger. And there's nothing more righteous in life than a furious counterattack against an evil person who's left us no choice. Ambivalence or vacillation in the face of unwarranted aggression is itself evil because cowardice is the opposite of love.

The truth is that no counterattack will work, regardless of the technical precision of the movements, if the person applying them isn't all in. Full commitment to the principles of self-defense must be trained just as much, if not more, than the physical attributes and technique. Technique without ferocity will fail.

And we have to say something else that should go without saying and that's this: if you aren't trying to take out the weakest targets while simultaneously defending your own, then you aren't doing martial arts. Period. You're doing something combative, yes, but not self-defense. And you must be doing this with gusto. By that we mean with full emotional commitment, not half-heartedly. Lots of people have a serious problem with being aggressive but curiously, not being bossy. In other words, they argue and whine, but recoil at the physical side of confrontation. As Bruce Lee said, either learn to endure or lead a less aggressive life. I can paraphrase that:

"STOP WHINING. *Always be respectful and mind your own business. Life is hard. Combat is really hard. Be ready. Be ready to hurt the bad guy and don't be of two minds about it.*"

I'VE BEEN CRITICIZED in the past over the utter brutality of this sort of thing. I've had people opine that it's barbaric. What's funny is that they miss the obvious. What they're saying, but are too smug and unrealistic to catch it, is that the means of stopping brutality ought really to be all warm and fuzzy. It shouldn't require *me* to be, well, you know...mean about it.

To paraphrase one of my favorite Bible verses, if I may: the end of the matter, all has been heard...we want to at least be just as mean as the enemy while also being 10 times as good. The goal of gaining skill isn't that it alleviates us from the responsibility of emotional content (of focused aggression). Skill is passion logically directed. Skill is the subordination of all parts into and for the aim of the whole. To think we can apply eye jabs and groin hits half-heartedly, therefore, is evidence of either our arrogance or ignorance. Soft target attacks aren't shortcuts; they're smart-cuts.

So, in summary, learn the whole system, be in functional shape so you can physically apply the system, and then, if you absolutely must defend yourself, apply the system with the utmost of moral anger.

7

CHI-SAO & GRAPPLING

The main idea (goal) of Wing Chun is to capture/control/destroy the enemy's central command unit (eyes, jaw, neck, throat, head). All other techniques and tactics are in service and, therefore, subordinate to this one. Other things are logically valid only insofar as this main goal is blocked for some reason.

I 'm gonna say something radical. Well, that is, at least according to the accepted logic of the day...and we know what I think of the anti-theoretical thinking of our time. Nevertheless, that said...here goes:

Wing Chun's Chi-sao training is grappling.

Yeah, I know. A word of explanation is in order.

First, in MMA it's common to speak of *stand-up training and grappling as separate disciplines.* Stand-up encompasses striking arts like boxing and Muay Thai in the main. Grappling, as the MMA training goes, is primarily freestyle wrestling, BJJ and Greco-Roman. These aren't all that's included, be sure, but nevertheless give us the skeleton of that beast which is the MMA fighter's arduous training. It's taken for granted that a fighter who's going to compete in the cage is going to have to do both - strike and grapple. The law of identity in logic dictates that all things that exist are *specific things* and not, nor can be, all things. Such it is with MMA...and Wing Chun too.

So, continuing with our theme of philosophical common sense, ground fighting and grappling are not the same thing. We all know that. We all know that grappling, insofar as it's understood by the UFC-influenced masses of our day, is a precarious bit business in an all-out violence scenario. Ground fighting in life-or-death altercations is wrought with peril. Let's look at this from the Wing Chun perspective, shall we?

The standard order of logic demands that we address reality as it is rather than how we'd like it to be. I'd like to be better looking, have more money and age a little backwards - kind of like *Benjamin Button* but with control. But reality is stubborn. Anyway, MMA and BJJ, for all their obvious benefits, carry with them a set of false beliefs. The easiest way to prove this is to consider the following points.

Imagine if tomorrow the UFC allowed groin strikes and eye-gouges.

Imagine if they allowed, say once per fight, similar to how other sports allow a limited number of challenges to a ref/ump's call, a cornerman could run in a take a shot at the opponent. Just once. The very threat of that would radically alter the strategies of ground fighting used by the competitors (not to mention who would be working in one's corner).

Or imagine that Dana White replaced mats with asphalt.

Imagine that instead of an empty octagon there were tables and chairs randomly placed in the cage.

Now, every rational person understands that any one of these rule changes would significantly alter MMA. If all of them were enacted, it would be Wing Chun.

Chi-sao is done in Wing Chun to teach us how to "grapple" - only we call it infighting because, for the aforementioned reasons, there's no such thing as strictly ground fighting. And we left out a good many variables the self-defender must consider. Weapons. Biting. Stairwells, countertops, curbs, cliffs, holes you could step in, and on and on. Real grappling as far as reality is concerned is "contact" range, where free movement is obstructed. And, again, reality always gets the last word. As I write this I'm surrounded by windows, hard floor, unforgiving countertops, and drywall. Chi-sao is the only "grappling" drill in which such things are taken into account. Striking any and every target is in play, and so is pushing, pulling, tripping, and throwing. In real fights, as Sifu Tony Massengill says, you hit people with things and things with people.

From 1914-1918 the Central and Allied powers traded millions of casualties for territory. The gains were often marked in feet, not miles. The trenches and barbed wire that marked the battlefields of Europe during the First World War were gone in the Second. Why?

Mobile armor made trench warfare less effective.

Indeed, military history shows this point over and over again. Bad generalship costs lives because it misunderstands the reality of the battlefield conditions. And that's our point about Chi-sao and grappling. We are grappling - but not in the way the modern fighter understands it...and that's because he's too sport focused, i.e., illogical.

Real fighting is our concern, not competition. The only trophy or prize the self-defender gets is what they already had in the first place, which is their safety and life. Sure, there's the honor that goes with not being a coward. That's certainly true and shouldn't be diminished in this age of moral confusion, but we're not talking about that. We're talking about material gain. "Winning" a self-defense fight means you aren't dead, maimed, left in a physically and/or emotionally dilapidated state, or raped. This means that the primary goal of self-defense is always and exactly that: defensive. For that reason, there are only two "ranges" of combat: free movement and contact.

In free movement we have no physical control over the enemy's striking ability. His balance is his. For that reason we must learn to use distance and angles in conjunction with our other tools so as to avoid his offense. An enemy who has his balance is dangerous. This can be seen as the *lin siu daai da* principle at work even absent direct contact with the enemy. Simultaneous defense and offense is literally always in play!

In contact phase we have some type of accountability of the enemy's weaponry. There will, of course, be varying degrees of control but the point is to use inside positioning/bridging in order to cut off and control their offense while simultaneously using our own.

Both of these "phases" must support one another and the skilled defender is a master at gaining and breaking contact to his/her advantage. *Thus, there is no "pure" ground fighting or pure striking element in all-out fighting.* It's a fight, for crying out loud and the stylized images floating in our minds, planted by cinema's artful choreography, or the sport world's adherence to rules, or the school's safe training environment, are all dangerous if we mistake them for reality. They aren't reality itself but, rather, *parts* of it which are isolated for education/training purposes[1]. Real-world violence, its nature, setting, and goal, are dissimilar to these things. We can be wrong or fuzzy on a good many things in life. The nature of violence isn't one of them. Not being sure what major to choose or being hazy on what married life will be like...sure, such will cause a little consternation here and there. But they won't kill you. Well, that is, of course, unless your definition of marriage includes other women and your wife's doesn't.

Yeah. That could get deadly.

Or if she expects that every Friday is Rom-Com movie date night. That might also kill you.

Okay. Back to the subject at hand.

Joking aside, false expectations about violence aren't something very funny, are they? That's how very, very bad things happen. Real violence is very swift and very brutal. It isn't academic or artful. It requires the utmost of simplicity and skill in the worst of scenarios.

To that end one of my most necessary duties as a martial art and self-defense instructor is to make sure I alert the student to this problem. Much of what we think we know about violence is polluted by the contradictions of sport, movie, and the dojo. And contradictions are evil things in a world where right action requires right thinking.

Think of fighting a little like the movie *The Martian*. When Matt Damon's character, Mark Whatley, was accidentally abandoned on Mars, with little hope of rescue, he had to figure out how to basically camp out on an alien planet hostile to human life. (In that way it was a little like going to the in-laws for the holidays). What Mark Whatley *thought* about reality absolutely had to correspond to what was or else he'd be dead in a hurry. Since the consequences were so dire - and readily apparent - part of the movie's drama was literally watching this process play out. Indeed, the "plot-theme" of the movie was *man's mind struggling to survive against nature*.

It's helpful, methinks, to approach self-defense this way too. A foolish miscalculation in fighting, though not easily as dangerous as life on Mars, may nevertheless end matters for us. Therefore, we should carefully test our thoughts and theories against the known principles so as to arrive at the correct plan of action. Elsewhere, I've referred to this as a philosophy of *principled-pragmatism*. In this book I've said it's a common-sense philosophical approach, borrowing from the Scottish common-sense realism school of thought and its primary advocate, Thomas Reid (1710-96).

In any event, the burden is always on us to adapt to reality, not the other way around. To discover "the best way" to survive and/or achieve a goal, like Mark Whatley on an alien planet, is the true goal of the mind, which is to say, adapt to reality. It's for this reason that we must always be humble and accept the burden of checking our premises. The whole idea of grappling, insofar as its understood in modern combat thinking, is compartmentalized, fragmented, and diluted by the sport world's rules and safety precautions.

The idea of "ranges" of fighting is an academic construct useful for training and tactical considerations. We may very well say that in real fighting there's only one range: danger. Any and all attempts to pigeonhole hand-to-hand violence omits or suppresses the common-sense reality that it's all fluid and happening extremely fast. Foul tactics, weapons, cluttered environments, and multiple opponents all make further classifications too daring as Bruce Lee once said.

Striking shouldn't be done at the expense of grappling nor vice-versa. Nothing can be done in a vacuum. Striking in a way that presumes having boxing gloves and hand-wraps is in contradiction to reality. People rarely have time to wrap their hands before a street-fight, after all. Just as well, grappling in a way that presupposes nice mats and all that is just as irrational. For training purposes, we must compartmentalize in order to develop skill but this compartmental-ization must not be done in contradiction to the primary goal. Inte-gration is the key. Lack of integration of the varied parts is dangerous. A logical systematic never plays one element over against another. For a system to be logical it must be both internally consis-tent and externally coherent with the facts of reality. Any contradic-tion proves fatal to a systematic's efficacy.

And this means that, properly understood, Wing Chun's Chi-sao is a grappling drill in that it works the contact phase of self-defense. Jim Driscoll, the great boxer who wrote *"The Straight Left & How to Cultivate It,"* which was a significant influence upon Bruce Lee and JKD, wrote that there's only two ways through a proper intercepting straight lead. One, you don't throw it; two you throw it with poor form. He also goes on to say that the clinch is an essential form of defense and footwork. On the first point, we wonder why we wouldn't throw it. Perhaps the opponent rushed in low or was able to disrupt our timing. And we wonder why he mentions clinching as a form of defense and footwork. The answer is something assumed in the Wing Chun systematic. People can close the gap fast. We can't "force our way out" but a strong opponent can force their way in. The clinch, as Driscoll calls it, is the infighting range of Wing Chun's Chi-sao.

Human beings in combat obviously can and do grab each other so there must be a logical means of understanding the best way of dealing with this for the purpose of self-defense, and then training it. We agree with Driscoll that the clinch is essential for defense when boxing. We also agree with MMA advocates and BJJ cultists (maybe a joke...maybe not) that everyone needs to know how to grapple. Where we disagree is with the precise definition. We consider, on the basis of logic (and common-sense realism) that fighting for one's life means that grappling is "contact" with the enemy. The objective is still to diminish his offensive capacity in the most economical and non-contradictory means possible. And we agree that infighters need to spar. We just disagree with the extreme sporting definition of sparring. We advocate for a robust Chi-sao curriculum as well as basic boxing.

THE GRAVE ERROR of the time, for Wing Chun students, is seeing Chi-sao only as a striking drill. This is the central reason why so many find it impossible to apply their Chi-sao in fighting and sparring. It's like preparing to hike the Appalachian Trail by learning to drive an off-road vehicle. Sure, you can drive your 4Runner in the woods but hiking the AT means exactly that: hiking. Likewise, contact training *includes striking but is grappling.*

Look at the Muay Thai clinch. It's actually the genius of that system. By controlling the head of the enemy, the Muay Thai fighter seeks to control their balance. And once they control their balance, they can strike, if not with impunity, then with relative safety. Muay Thai's clinch and Wing Chun's bridge control have much more in common than the average Wing Chun student likes to think. Muay Thai fighters have to adjust their habits once they go into MMA because of the takedowns. But, as we've pointed out, the cage itself, and the rules applied therein, make it so that grappling styles have an advantage in the cage. If the Muay Thai fighter could eye-gouge and headbutt, for example, their clinch fighting would be even more effective in the cage and they'd likely require less BJJ.

This is the best way to look at the issue. Imagine Wing Chun as a "dirty" form of Muay Thai. I know...this can be a dangerous oversimplification but the principles in play are instructive so that we understand the point. If a Muay Thai fighter grabs a guy and pulls him into a knee, that's likely to end matters right there. For our purposes we don't like the emphasis on head control only, thereby leaving the enemy's hands free. In self-defense, that might be a significant problem. Though he might very well be off balance, he still might be able to pull a weapon. *But that's literally the type of control the Wing Chun fighter should have over the balance of the enemy!* Most Muay Thai fighters have a better clinch/inside game than Wing Chun fighters because the latter is focused only on the hands and striking and hardly at all upon balance. And controlling the balance literally is grappling insofar as self-defense is concerned because an off-balance enemy has a severely reduced offensive capacity. Thus, in common sense Wing Chun, we want to do that by *attacking* the head/face/neck while simultaneously taking their balance and controlling their hands. This is all done by applying the principles and core structures of Wing Chun dynamically. And the only way to learn this is by doing the forms properly and then learning the proper (read that: logically progressive) Chi-sao curriculum with skillful classmates.

Okay, let's put it another way. When we're at close-range, hitting/striking an opponent *without* simultaneously taking or disturbing their balance is less efficient than doing both at the same time. The Wing Chun systematic and structures provide us with the means of doing both, so we should use them. An eye-gouge, for example, using the *fook-sao* structure as developed in the forms and through drills, give us the ability to both attack the eyes and take/disrupt the balance of the enemy. And it does this because the fook-sao structure is logically integrated into the stance-footwork. Furthermore, the shape of the attack and its integration provides defensive coverage too.

So, you see, it's not just "oh, it's a fight, so go for their eyes."

There's a system in play and the parts must not contradict the whole - and the training drills must integrate as well, which is exactly why Chi-sao is a type of grappling drill provided our definition of grappling is consistent with self-defense reality. If we see it as an MMA thing, or a wrestling match, then, no, Chi-sao is certainly not grappling. It simply depends upon what the standard is that we're applying.

A balanced opponent is dangerous. If they have their balance we should try and be in a position, or at a distance, where reaching us is difficult. A fencer uses range carefully. A gunfighter/soldier uses cover and concealment carefully. So should every fighter. Not taking steps to thwart the enemy's offense through careful positioning and range is foolhardy. It's a careful study unto itself (hence why we refer to Bruce Lee's JKD as Chi-sao without the touch).

At very close range, however, such distance and positioning that negates the enemy's offense is hard to achieve. This is why all valid close-range sport fighting systems include clinching and grappling! Controlling the balance of the enemy and/or smothering his attack is the key at close range. Wing Chun fighters should recognize this and use it as an interpretive guide for how they understand, train, and apply their close-quarter skills.

To that end, it's logical to say that truly scientific close-range fighting includes pushing-pulling-striking-shifting-stepping. Not only that, a close-range fighting systematic must have all these aspects *equally* integrated. Granted, an individual student of the system will very likely excel, with training, at one or two aspects over the others, and have their personal passions and all that. But this would in no wise mean that the system itself would suffer from incoherence or contradiction, merely that the student of the system, the human being, would introduce the so-called human factor into the equation. I have trained a student that was massive. He was the size of an NFL lineman and could bench press a small village. His application of the Wing Chun system, therefore, leaned heavily upon his extraordinary strength and not so much on lightning-fast kicks. A valid fighting systematic will always be individually applicable.

Nevertheless, whether a student personally focuses more on one aspect of Wing Chun or not isn't the point. The issue at hand is that Wing Chun is not primarily a striking art; it's a fighting art, which means, it's an integrated systematic that includes:

STRIKING - WITH ALL/ANY valid weapon (kicks, punches, knees, elbows, stomps, head butts, finger jabs/gouges/rakes, etc.

FOOTWORK & shifting that safely positions the basic structure of the YJKYM

PUSHING and pulling

THROWING and sweeping

BREAKING and locking

SO, is Wing Chun a grappling art? Yes. And a striking one too. All of that should be baked into the cake. Our current understanding of grappling is contradictory in that it's hyper-specialized in a way that's inconsistent with the realities of all-out combat.

WITH ALL THAT SAID, here are some grappling basics Wing Chun students should practice in their Chi-sao curriculum. We note that the student shouldn't see this as grappling and the previously presented material as striking due to the fact that the strikes were delivered in a manner that simultaneously disrupted the enemy's balance. We ask the reader to refer back to the photos of your author grabbing Aaron's eyes and shoving Devin's head into the hard wall. That's the primary thing we intend to do. These are auxiliary actions.

CHI-SAO GRAPPLING BASICS

THE SIDE STRANGLE

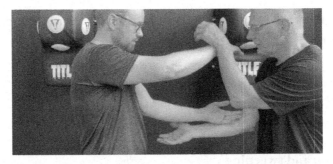

Grappling, locking, and throwing can easily be added to our Chi-sao training (and should be). Here I use the Huen-sao with my right to gain the outside line.

But as Elliot is trying to move with me, he brings his arm up to push at me. Again, sorry that a book can't perfectly show the sequence but I'm sure you get the idea. Not everyone is going to react the same way, incidentally. With some, basic striking is the key; with others, like here, it's grappling. The rule is: let them help you hurt them.

In the previous photo you notice that I "cleared" the other hand, using the Guan-Huen principle. This allowed me to "throw" Elliot's pressure to the side and then use the Tok-Sao under his elbow to pop-up his left arm. Now in this photo I'm stepping in to take advantage of the opening.

Stepping in I apply a side-strangle or, for you BJJ folks out there (as if you're reading a Wing Chun book, but I digress) an arm triangle. This type of grappling has its place and should be a part of everyone's Wing Chun curriculum. The action of closing the left arm (as I'm doing here) is used in the SLT form as you bring your double Faak-sao movements back to the Lan-sao position. Focus on the energy moving forward as though you're close-lining or choking someone. You see? Wing Chun is incredibly diversified. Hopefully, this gives you a whole new appreciation of the forms.

This time I'm gonna go the other way. This often happens when the opponent is taller than you and is pushing a lot (with static energy).

By extending his energy (pressure) too far, Elliot allows me to scoot to the angle and pop his right elbow up using Tok-sao.

At that point I close the gap and execute the strangle. To finish the hold you can close your hands or use the non-choking hand (in this case, my left) to pull the other wrist. The strangle works by squeezing and eliminating any space between you and the enemy.

THE ARM DRAG

Another move that's effective is the arm-drag. I start with the Huen-sao in order to gain outside wrist control with my right.

As we continue to roll, I execute a cross-grab (similar to the opening hand grabbing action in the Chum Kiu form) to grab Elliot's left arm with my right.

I now have wrist and elbow control

I pull using energy from both hands. Never pull anyone toward you. Down and away works like a charm, which, incidentally, is shown on the Wooden Dummy in the form's first section.

Just because we use a grappling technique doesn't mean we have to continue grappling, throwing or locking. In this case, the arm drag merely clears the line and off-balances Elliot enough so that I can strike. Remember: "listen" to your enemy. Cooperate with him to his demise.

Arm Drag & Shoulder Lock

We're back in the momma-poppa positions.

This time I execute the arm drag without using Huen-sao first. From the top position (Bong-sao) I use an inner wrist grab and pull down as my left hand grabs Elliot's tricep just above the elbow.

This sequence happens all as one. The grab, turn, and pull happen simultaneously. Practice slowly at first so that you get smooth. Never be in a hurry and be ready to strike should the opponent make an adjustment. Everything in Wing Chun is integrated.

In this position you can see that I'm ready to hit him. But in some cases you might not want to pummel your opponent. Imagine a drunken knucklehead or crazy uncle...something that requires control rather than extreme violence.

In that event, I shoot my right hand under Elliot's left to execute a shoulder lock. A move like this is possible when the enemy is off-balance and flailing. I wouldn't consider it a primary move but it's a helpful part of our tool-box in less than life-or-death scenarios.

My position is the key. By being off Elliot's center I have options should he be able to turn back to face me.

At this point I can throw Elliot into things, knee him, or even stomp his ankle or knee. As always, don't forget that getting a shoulder lock can happen in a variety of ways. We're using Chi-sao as a training device. The goal isn't Chi-sao, it's efficiency in close-quarter combat. That said, you'd be surprised how an arm-drag and/or shoulder-lock can come available when someone is trying to defend themselves against striking.

Arm Drag & Rear Choke

Again, we'll start by using the arm-drag action.

Pulling Elliot off-balance, his back is exposed.

I step through and execute a rear-choke. A thing to note is that for all-out fighting, our grappling maneuvers must not be such a technique that prohibits us from quickly disengaging should another opponent enter the fray. For this reason also, our vision and mobility must be maintained so that we can keep watch on our flank. You don't need to take a sucker-punch from some opportunistic fellow. Many contemporary grappling moves are suicidal versus more than one opponent and we must have the muscle-memory/options to strike, push, pull, etc., to avoid tying ourselves up with a single foe if another is ready to jump in.

Head & Arm Throw

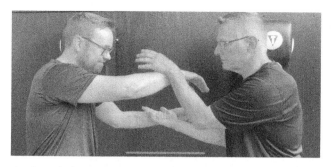

From the basic position I step in and use a variation of the inside hand/Taan-sao attack.

This is basically the same action seen in the Wooden Dummy form's first section. If the opponent moves his head away from a strike we can simply continue the striking hand action and use it as a controlling hand/neck-grab. Combined with arm control, we pull him down and to the side.

This can be a full-on throw to the ground, a smash into a wall or counter-top or car door, or a segue to a knee strike. It simply depends upon the situation and the opponent's reaction.

Lop-Sao & Arm Break

We say again that basics are there for a reason. Though we shouldn't be chained (as my Sifu likes to call it) to the "momma-poppa" positions, nor should we jettison them. Why? Because of the problem of extremes. On one hand we can become too literal...a Wing Chun legalist; on the other hand we can become an anarchist, using freedom as an excuse for sloppiness.

Often times the enemy is pressing a hand, trying to overpower you. In many Wing Chun schools they frown on the type of pressing and static force that non-Wing Chun fighters often use. Granted, to use such energy is "bad" Wing Chun. That's true but since it's the most common energy we're going to face (hence the pressure drill too, by the way) it's important that we learn to deal with it systematically. Against Elliot's attempt to overpower me, my basic structure holds until such a moment as he's too committed to the line. At that point I shift and attack his extended arm.

Lop-sao is often combined with a strike but in reality the enemy's force often carries them past the striking line and off-angle. An attack on the elbow works nicely with Lop-sao, therefore, as it takes advantage of what non-Wing Chun fighters often do. In this case, I use the Jum-sao action (sinking elbow) with my right as I pull with my Lop-sao. In practice we must be very, very careful as it's easy to severely injure your partner's arm here.

You can use this as a submission but if done with extreme speed and violence it's a breaking action. The action is also reminiscent of the "freeing hand" action at the end of the SLT form just before the chain-punch sequence. In fact, this is the essence of using two-way energy...for breaking. Chin-Na (to capture and control/destroy) is baked into the cake of Wing Chun.

PULL/PUSH

Another thing to remember about in-fighting is the efficacy of pushing and pulling. One of the best ways of dealing with tension from the enemy is to use the pull-push principle. Let the enemy go where he wants...but help him along. If Elliot is pushing forward...

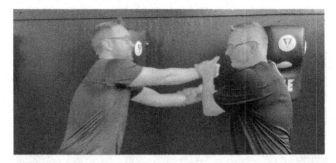

...I can shift and pull to the side. This is picking up on the very first drill we did: learning to shift when the enemy pushes too much. The pulling action along with the shift sends Elliot forward almost like he was pushing against a door I suddenly opened.

Often times the opponent will try and catch themselves, correcting their balance. If they do this, push into their center-of-mass as they try and bring themselves back to scratch. The effect of the stepping push along with their transfer of weight can be catastrophic.

In this photo I show how shoving people into things is a great tool. In real fights there are hard "borders" everywhere. Countertops, cars, hard walls...that sort of thing. By taking control of Elliot's center-of-gravity I can slam him into hard things. A lot of Wing Chun fighters falsely believe that they must chain-punch everything that isn't nailed down. But the truth is that the system has a variety of tools. The pushing hands, as well as the Jut and Lop for jerking/pulling people off balance are ignored at our peril. Wing Chun fighters should in no way be one-trick ponies.

THIS ISN'T a comprehensive list of the grappling that's available to us in Chi-sao. For example, we didn't cover seizure, control, and breaking of small joints, nor throws, trips, and sweeps. That would require another volume. Nevertheless, what we've detailed is the foundation of those things. Again: grappling, locking, throwing, breaking, etc., are all part of the larger whole. Also, this shows that, like sparring, there are many valid uses of the Chi-sao drill. The goal of Chi-sao isn't Chi-sao! The goal is proficiency in all that in-fighting entails. This means that there's no one ubiquitous manner of doing the drill and doing that will necessarily hamper one's in-fighting education, even destroy it.

Indeed, there will be times where our primary goal of attacking and controlling the head of the enemy is achieved forthwith. Other times we may need another tactic - perhaps we need to pin the enemy against a wall and then deliver a heavy kick to his knee or ankle. Or, perhaps, as one of our students has experienced due to his job, that using grappling holds is the primary thing since he has to subdue people. In all, we must learn to use Chi-sao and Wing Chun, not be used by them.

Lastly, in light of the material presented in this chapter especially, we need to remember the simplicity of Wing Chun. Our goal should never to be complication for the sake of it. That's usually the result of men and women living too long in a luxury where they aren't tested. The brutal reality of combat is seen in this chapter's first photo. The thing is, mistakes happen...and sometimes the unexpected has a way of challenging us. This is why Wing Chun is *simply comprehensive* or *comprehensively simple.* A good pilot has the experience and knowledge to handle extreme conditions but we hope every flight is routine. It's the same here.

8

BOXING & WING CHUN...BUT WHAT KIND OF BOXING?

*I*t's clear that your author is making a rather bold claim about Wing Chun in general and Chi-sao in particular. To support this claim please indulge me a historical example in order to show that what we think we're seeing today in the sporting/combat world isn't exactly accurate.

IT'S SAID that the great John L. Sullivan was the last bare-knuckle heavyweight champion of the world. Though this is true in point of fact, as he did indeed defeat Jake Kilrain in all that oppressive Mississippi heat in July of 1889 over 75 rounds of bare-knuckle combat, Sullivan was no fan. He preferred, it should be known, the Marquis of Queensbury rules - you know, the modern rules.

What does this have to do with Wing Chun? Hang on. Trust me...there's a payoff coming on this.

You see, Sullivan's fame throughout his decade long run as the heavyweight champion wasn't due to his circumspect personality and self-control. In fact, the man's behavior was nothing short of barbaric. His drunken carousing, cussing, fighting, arguing, bombast, inconsistency, and all-around general savagery - and this during the height of the "Oh, I never...!" Victorian era - was well known by all.

Think about this for a second. In an era unparalleled for its self-righteousness, John L. Sullivan openly ran with women who weren't his wife. He was, as champion of the world, also the world's best-known drunk. He was so bad that even the worst frat-boy would say, "whoa, dude...chill out." When he was sent a cable that his dear mother was gravely ill it took him *months* to clear his party schedule and finally go see her. He made it before she died, by the way. Just barely. He stayed for a few hours, then went back out to party. Then she died. Seriously.

Oh, and if that wasn't bad enough, when the great pugilist was touring America on the great Knockout Tour where he netted something like $150,000 (at a time when a nice house could be bought for around $1,000), he received word that his only son had suddenly taken ill.

His boy died.

John never went home.

And all this was public knowledge courtesy of the newspapers that followed his every move.

Sullivan was such a reprobate, made so by his aggression and alcoholism, that he burned through every single business relationship he had during his career too.

So, how does such a lout have a loyal following in a time like that? How does Victorian America put up with such a man? Simple.

Because he could knock out everyone.

Times haven't changed all that much in one respect, right? I mean, Mike Tyson bit off a piece of Evander Holyfield's body in a prize fight - deliberately spitting out his mouthpiece and then chowing down. Let the horror of that sink in. Imagine for a moment the real absurdity of it. Imagine such a thing in any other line of work. If one salesman at a dealership got into a fight with another that would be bad enough, right? Arguments happen all the time over who gets the next customer that walks through the door, after all. But a fight? But what would happen if one sales guy chomped off another's ear?

Tyson did in the ring what's unthinkable in the ethos of the ring. Sure, we tolerate aggression but there's an almost sacred nature to the adherence to the rules in the ring. To bite off Holyfield's ear! It's almost like the salesman losing a sale and then, in frustration and vengeance, destroying the car rather than letting the customer have it. Such an attack is not just on the car but on the profession itself.

But Tyson, like John L. Sullivan, got away with it - albeit after some perfunctory posturing by the "governing bodies" - because the public was fascinated by him. And why? Because of his power.

You see, America then, was so prim and proper that they wouldn't loosen their collars or take off a tie while suffering heat stroke standing outside with no shade, in triple digit Mississippi heat, watching Sullivan batter Kilrain. Isn't that amazing? The fact of the matter is that the thousands that witnessed the match 104 miles north of New Orleans on Colonel Charles Rich's property in Rich-burg, Mississippi were breaking the law. Bare-knuckle boxing was illegal in all 38 states at that time. Governor Lowry of Mississippi opposed the fight and even had state trooper guarding the border with Louisiana. All the spectators left on a special train from New Orleans with no idea where they were actually going and the conductor blew right past the "road block" set by the governor.

Local sheriff W. J. Cowart stepped in the ring before it started and half-heartedly commanded everyone to leave, declaring it an unlawful assembly. Considering that everyone there was armed - including the famous gunfighter Bat Masterson - his threat had no teeth. One of Sullivan's backers slipped the sheriff a few hundred dollars (almost a year's income back then) and he went and took a seat.

So, all this law-breaking and duplicity and yet, despite the temperature being 104, no one, ladies included, would shed clothing to cool down. Ah, those Victorian codes! That's the thing that concerns us here. The fact is that everyone there was openly and willfully breaking the law, flaunting it, snubbing it...and they didn't care, so long as they did it together. But the social law of modesty was enforced and no one would break it despite Sullivan and Kilrain beating the bejabbers out of each other while half naked.

See where we're going?

Maybe this will help: we often miss the obvious because we're focused on the wrong thing. Enamored by Sullivan's power, they were willing to overlook all the laws that got in the way of seeing that power on display. The dress code stayed in place because in their minds those were separate issues. If they started to shed clothing to cool down that would have meant, in their minds, a complete repudiation of morality and that's not what they thought they were doing.

Well, just as they missed the irony of all that, we miss the obvious too. John L. Sullivan didn't like the bare-knuckle rules. Those were, of course, the London Prize Ring rules. First, the bare-knuckle business got him in legal hassles. That's true. But the bigger issue was that the London Prize Ring rules made the game harder for a power puncher.

Our point emerges. (Thanks for staying with me...and if you skimmed, shame on you! You missed some utterly fascinating history. And there were jokes about commies and pictures of puppies. Seriously...go back and check.)

The London rules allowed for throws and greater use of infighting. A bare-handed fighter couldn't throw the all-out bombs for not only fear of breaking his hands but also because massive weight shifts would leave him vulnerable to grappling. Oh, and another little piece of historical info that concerns us Wing Chun fighters is that there were no mats in those rings. Getting tossed onto a grass surface is a whole lot better than being slammed to asphalt, sure, but still not as nice as state-of-the-art grappling mats.

I once had a BJJ instructor ask to teach some classes out of my school. The room I had available had mats - striking mats, that is. They were thin. He passed on the opportunity because he said it would be too train to train on such thin mats. Sullivan and Kilrain would've scoffed.

So, yeah, we're conveniently forgetting that old-school boxing was far more MMAish than we think. And because of this it's a link to how we see Wing Chun. The punches were shorter and straighter and thrown more from the clinch. There was careful adherence to keeping your balance because getting thrown hard might result - and sometimes did - in broken wrists, arms, ribs, and separated shoulders. Sometimes, as Sullivan did against Kilrain, a fighter might "accidentally" drop a knee on the fallen foe too - making it look like he lost his balance and couldn't help himself.

In fact, Sullivan suffered a broken forearm in a previous bareknuckle encounter because the opponent was adept at using his elbows and head on defense. In the modern rules, Sullivan's enormous blows, full of KO power, were protected by the gloves and rules. Under the London rules, however, his opponent could use that power against him. To say it again: John L. Sullivan, despite being considered the last bare-knuckle champion, hated fighting under the London rules because KO's were easier and safer for him under the gloved rules. This is all to say that the London Prize ring rules were/are more commensurate with Wing Chun than modern boxing.

One last thing.

Before John's historic match with Jake Kilrain his life of dissipation and debauchery almost caught up to him. He nearly died in the late summer-early fall the year before. Hedonism will do that to a man.

Enter Willam Muldoon.

Muldoon was the Greco-Roman Wrestling champion of America at the time. An ardent believer in what was called *muscular Christianity,* Muldoon was quite famous for his accomplishments. Of course, his acclaim was nowhere near Sullivan's due to the aforementioned fact that KO's are always more fun to watch than wrestling matches... something of which that Dana White surely understands too. One of Muldoon's matches lasted, gasp, seven hours!

So, why would Sullivan go and train under a wrestler for a boxing match? You see, here we are again. It's easy to miss the obvious. Boxing and wrestling were quite a bit more intertwined then - just as

I'm claiming they are in Wing Chun. The rules, which made the boxing game easier on the eyes (read that: more profitable) separated them. A culture that could listen to the Lincoln-Douglas debate had an expectation vastly different than our own. A two-hour match between Sullivan and Kilrain would bore us to death. Lots of *grappling* from the stand-up position was the norm. Imagine Greco-Roman wrestling and compact boxing in one package and you get the idea.

Muldoon whipped big John into shape on his famous farm in upstate New York. Long walks (12 miles a day), a simple diet, jumping rope, Greco-Roman wrestling, hitting the bag, and light sparring brought Sullivan back to form before the Kilrain fight. In fact, Sullivan and Muldoon did an exhibition wrestling bout on May 28 of that year. Interestingly, the rules used to govern it were the London Prize Ring rules. This means that they fought on the inside and wrestled without striking (no striking because it was just an exhibition).

This informs us as to what Wing Chun and Chi-sao are and ought to be. Sure, Wing Chun is its own thing – more logical and exact than London Prize Ring boxing – but not wholly different.

Isn't history fun?

9

BRUCE LEE & WING CHUN

I t's said that Bruce Lee's *Jeet Kune Do* is Chi-sao without the touch. I've always been intrigued by that statement and think, after a number of years reflecting upon it, that there's more to it then we're tempted to believe.

First, let it be said that your author still believes firmly that Lee was a Wing Chun man and did not, repeat not, repudiate his martial heritage. I know that in some circles that's like saying Donald Trump wasn't a bad president and sure to elicit crazed howls of protest. But the fact is that both the structural framework and philosophical core of JKD are, in point of fact, consistent with those of his mother system.

In a letter he wrote to his mentor, Wong Shun Leung, Lee approvingly mentions both boxing and Wing Chun and thanks both Wong and Master Ip for having set him on a practical path. Granted, Lee was saying that he'd made changes along this practical path but they were, when studied objectively, tactical modifications of the aforementioned structural foundation he already had. In light of this I think we're still catching up and extrapolating upon much of Lee's work.

Why? Was Lee such a genius? Perhaps. I think the clearer

answer is, though, that he asked the big questions. He dared. He wasn't complacent. Physically and philosophically he took very little for granted - and that's a very, very hard thing to do. Those bloviators on social media that bash the late Mr. Lee, deriding him as a "fake fighter" because he never competed according to their modern standards, have not an inch of his philosophical vitality. Lee wasn't a "second-hander" as the late author Ayn Rand would have described them, living on the scraps of thoughts of other men, and most times hardly scraps, but fetid refuse long discarded. Lee's mind was, if not original in thought (as James Bishop's work has proven that he was a middleman of truth rather than a producer of it) at least a lover of it. What a great thing to be said about any man!

Also, in light of Mr. Bishop's scrutiny of Lee's intellectual heritage, and the plagiarism issues aside, we do well to remember that the late martial artist was that first - a martial artist - and also an actor/director/screenwriter. It's fair to say that he was an artist of high order and his body of work left in cinema testifies to his skill. Arguably, we never would have seen the stylistic beauties of violence in *The Matrix* unless Lee had come first.

Every life is full of those interesting riddles we might call contradictions but are often times, in point of fact, and seen with tolerance and experience, the arc of their personal story. Those that deify Lee do themselves great harm; those that dismiss his efforts and production offhand without serious consideration also injure themselves for the simple reason that the questions Lee wrestled with are those that concern us all.

Simplicity and directness are complex subjects. Unity and diversity are always hanging around, standing there unimpressively, seemingly innocuous, and minding their own business, with hardly any admirable muscle mass whatsoever. Despite their mundane appearance, they're the greatest philosophical opponents of all. They knock out all challengers and continue to overpower the most robust intellects of every generation. They're huge subjects hiding in plain sight. A man who gets into the ring with a great champion and finds himself at last overmatched is lauded, is he not? In boxing we rightly applaud the loser of a great fight against another great fighter. Joe Frazier lost to a great Ali and so on. Well, such it should be, methinks, that we should think of Bruce Lee in many respects. He stepped into the ring to try to understand the paradoxes of *one-and-many*, he threw his hat in the ring against how simplicity in a world of a million particulars can possibly make sense. This is what I mean to say when I say that he dared. To step in the ring against a human opponent requires a certain courage, yes; but to seek the truth seriously and humbly, the whole truth, is another form of grit altogether.

It's to this that we look at his *Jeet Kune Do* and how it relates to Wing Chun and our specific subject.

The plainness of the facts clear away the debris that builds up on the runways of our mind, clearing us to get above the field - to take a look from above. Let's do that, shall we?

Lee only trained formally in martial arts in the Wing Chun system. He did this as a busy teenage boy. This fact screams at us because for anyone to insist that there's no difference between a man at 16 and the same man at 30 is sheer evidence of insanity. Or the critic is himself 16 and can't fathom the realities of age and experience. The raw material and seeds of interpretation planted in young Bruce Lee were those of Wing Chun - specifically by both Ip Man and Wong Shun Leung. This fact is further shown by David Peterson's book on his teacher, Wong Shun Leung, *Beyond the Pointing Finger - the Combat Philosophy of Wong Shun Leung*. In short, Peterson's book, unwittingly for sure, may be the best JKD book you'll ever read!

You see, Ip Man never wrote a book and what we know of his overall philosophy of fighting and training is second-hand. Let that sink in. We have to take the word of students and this word is, quite naturally, filtered down through their own process of interpretation. In a class of many students, a teacher's message will fall upon minds that see the same things through a variety of interpretive lenses. An electrician and a novelist will both hear the same message, receive the same drills, and then filter the information back to the next generation differently. Even two police officers will do this. For example, an undercover narcotics detective and a traffic cop, though both in the same profession technically, will see the information differently.

We all have a presuppositional interpretive standard at the bottom of our reasoning. Ignoring this is foolish - as well as the root of most of human misery. An undercover detective will view combat much differently than a boxer. A SWAT sniper's view of guns is different than that detective since both, by professional tactical engagement necessity, have vastly dissimilar uses of a firearm - both in type, range, and timing.

Okay, so Wong Shun Leung's combat philosophy gives us amazing insight - the best, frankly - into the garden soil in which young Lee's mind sprung and was nourished. It's clear from Peterson's book, a true and undeniable treasure, that WSL's insistence upon simplicity, practicality, adaptability reigned supreme. That Ip Man and WSL were not authoritarian in their teaching, but men of ideas and principles, is abundantly clear in Peterson's book. In fact, there are some pages where one wonders if what they're reading was written by Lee himself. Such is the similarity of presuppositions.

Sifu David Peterson with two dummies...one of which is the author at Greenville Academy back in 2014. Meeting Sifu David was a true blessing as he's a gifted teacher and practitioner of Wong Shun Leung Ving Tsun. Not only that but he's very giving of his vast knowledge and this particular dummy gained quite a bit from him. His books, as mentioned, are some of the best - if not the best - books ever written on our beloved fistic science.

The other thing to note about Lee's Wing Chun origin is that a great teacher's message is lost on the vast majority of his students. Many of the things Ip Man advised his students were radical in light of the traditions of the time. To tell a student, "don't take my word for it...make sure you test it out," isn't something that catches us as odd in our hyper-individualistic culture. But you simply didn't question your elders then – and certainly not in China.

It's clear that WSL and his star pupil, Lee, weren't common minds. They were philosopher-fighters; they were men of the mind as well as the fist. Such men of the mind are rare and I strongly suspect that's the major reason behind why some Wing Chun (and JKD) is so different (dare we say inferior?) to others. A "concrete bound" student of Wing Chun is going to have a hard time understanding the abstractions of the philosophical and tactical points. Such a thinker needs to be told what to do; they see everything in mechanical terms.

Every class I teach has a mix of people not merely with physical variances - some tall, others short and so on - but emotional/intellectual too. Some are more aggressive than others, of course. Some people have a very hard time loosening up. We all know this but fail to consider the implications. A rational system is able to teach all of these people, despite their variations, how best to use their body for the purpose of self-defense. Just as well, it (the system of logic) provides the tactical liberty for these unique individuals to specialize in certain aspects of the systematic.

This is what I mean when I say that JKD is, most succinctly put, *Bruce Lee Wing Chun.* If there's WSL Wing Chun, and Ip Man Wing Chun, and so on, which is all to say application interpretations of the Wing Chun system, then JKD fits that mold. If Wing Chun, in its forms and drills, provides for us an instrument, like a guitar, then one's use of that instrument doesn't change the guitar into a bass.

There's a great scene in *Back to the Future* that illustrates the point. After Marty McFly goes all rock-n-roll crazy at the *Enchantment Under the Sea* dance, playing a **style** of guitar no one had heretofore heard, he hands the instrument back to Marvin Berry, the guitar's owner. Berry looks at the guitar as if it's some alien thing, nearly afraid of it. He's in awe. His expression is exactly that which is worn when someone does something in a manner previously thought impossible.

Lee, the artist and philosopher, handed the guitar back to us and said, "see what we can do with this thing?"

It's all too tempting to give in to the fear. It's all too tempting to cast the whole thing from one's mind rather than think it through. Bruce Lee didn't break the mold of Wing Chun. Instead, he showed what it was capable of. He lived out his teachers' foundational charge to him, which was "don't be the slave of Wing Chun...make it your slave." In that way, Bruce Lee's journey to *Jeet Kune Do* was exactly that which WSL and Ip Man had prepared him to do. The personal journey of Lee would have been vastly different had he stayed in Hong Kong and finished training in the Wing Chun system, sure. But, as testimony to his dedication and intellectual honesty, he kept working toward the goal.

Lee's *Jeet Kune Do* seeks to intercept the attack with a scientifically superior counterattack. If JKD is, therefore, simply to simplify, as Lee often stated, then the *Jeet* concept is the linchpin of the whole shebang – unifying the theoretical and practical. He was up against the great philosophical conundrum of "one-and-many." How to make sense of simplicity in a world full of variables is the challenge. The manner in which to do this, the only way, is to have a system of principles and concepts, not just techniques. In this way, the *Jeet* idea (or concept), done often at long-range in JKD, is Lee's application of the *lin siu daai da* principle of Wing Chun. The interception idea is logical insofar as it combines defense and offense. Simplification is achieved through the correct understanding of the principles and then the non-contradictory application of them by individuals using techniques that express and conform to that truth. Chi-sao is an application drill of *lin siu daai da* and JKD's interception is Bruce Lee's use of that principle in a way that suited him. Simultaneous attack and defense is the key.

LAST POINT.

When you watch basketball today you're invariably going to see a different game than was played in the 90's. The main difference is the volume of 3-pointers attempted. The catalyst of this was Steph Curry, a relatively small sharpshooter whose long-range mastery showed everyone what was possible. Lumbering big men playing as close to the basket is out right now and quick-release shots from beyond are in thanks to Steph Curry maximizing his potential. Everyone saw it and went, "wow, I never thought of that before."

It's still the same game, just played differently now. The structures and fundamentals are identical but the strategy and tactics are changed. In that way, Lee's JKD is Steph Curry's NBA. Steph still drives to the basket now and then and, yes, Jordan and Bird shot some threes back in the day.

These aren't perfect analogies, but I humbly submit that this is the proper relationship between Wing Chun and JKD. Learn the forms and drills – especially Chi-sao just like you'd learn the guitar or how to dribble and shoot. Then, according to your attributes, maximize your performance and don't be a slave to only one tactical interpretation of how to use those fundamentals. The system is yours. It belongs to you, not you to it. You don't owe your life to Wing Chun (or JKD) but are using it to save your life. If you want to play country music with your guitar, though for the life of me I've no idea why any sane person would, that's your choice. Be the best country guitar player you can be.

This is what having no way as way means. Logically, it's an artistic/poetic expression of tactical application freedom. Contrary interpretations succeed only in annihilating the systematic of Wing Chun.

10

KEEP IT SIMPLE: THE BRUTAL TRUTH

L isten, it doesn't make me joyous to have to include something like this. I'd rather not. And please don't think I'm trying to rub your face in it. The thing is, there's a reality to violence that many of us, by virtue of our virtues, aren't required to face every day. And even in Wing Chun class where we're practicing self-defense violence, respect and control are emphasized.

They must, of course. I mean, after all, if we didn't do that the classes would be awfully short. And there'd be all those pesky conversations with the police...and lawyers.

Since it's loss of self-control and the refusal to show respect to others (this includes everyone...Democrats and Republicans!) that causes violence in the first place, a martial art school is morally obligated to teach these virtues. A school of martial art in which self-control and respect aren't paramount is like a fireman who's also an arsonist.

Anyway, the point is that civilization can make us weak in the way that a man can fall into habits of leisure, start putting on the pounds, and suddenly find himself comfortably out of shape. Yep, we can go from dad-bod to downright bad-bod in no time. If everyone is nice all the time, and the economy is good, people can slip into the false belief that *everyone is literally nice*. But the hard truth is that mankind has a serious problem with violence and oppression. Every culture. Every tribe. Every race. Violence, crime and tyranny are man's default setting. This is quite sad, yes, but invariably and unarguably true.

Being fat and happy doesn't alter the facts of reality.

It's sort of like the famous Rocky Balboa story in *Rocky III*. Having become champion of the world, Rocky's sudden wealth drew him into a life of leisure that he'd simply never been able to afford in the past. Mr. T's hyper-aggressive Clubber Lang, Rocky's number one challenger, suffered from no such thing. He was hungry. He was all in. While Rocky was kissing babies for all the adoring fans at his training camp, Clubber was pounding out angry reps.

And speaking of training camps, Rocky was set up in a hotel ball-room full of dancing girls and music. It was more like a boxing Disney than a training camp. There were distractions galore. Clubber, though it was never shown completely, appeared to be training in a cellar somewhere. Rocky was always surrounded by people...non-boxing people. Autograph seekers were everywhere. Clubber was always depicted alone. Of course, anyone with rudimentary boxing knowledge knows he must have had trainers, but the movie's director made sure that the contrast was painfully clear.

Rocky was civilized and distracted. He'd become supremely nice. He'd lost the hunger and focus that had compelled him to the championship. His opponent, though, was as focused as a ferocious beast on the hunt. As the movie put it - and the famous song enshrined in our memory from 1982 - one had *the eye of the tiger* and the other didn't.

As for our subject, there's a saying that comes to mind: mean beats good when good isn't mean.

Yes, we should and must be men and women of honor. We should love our neighbor as we love ourselves. We should be gentle and meek with the power and skill we develop. But when it's time for battle the loving thing is to "abhor what is evil." Abhorrence of the evil of immoral aggression is both ethical and loving. The fact of these two things - aggressiveness and love - are not, contrary to popular opinion, antithetical in the heart of the disciplined martial artist. Aggressiveness without love is barbarism; love without aggressiveness toward evil (insofar as the issue of self-defense is concerned) is at best sentimentalism, not love. At worst it's cowardice. A trained, focused, and ferocious response to the evil of aggression is not, repeat not, antithetical to sound character. In biblical history we see Abraham with his 318 trained men rise up to deliver his beloved nephew, Lot, from slavery. Samson, despite his prolific problems with women, was a master of violence. If the Bible had *Avengers* Samson would have been *Captain Israel.* King David was a mighty warrior even before the famous clash with Goliath. Oh...and let's not forget Jesus Himself grabbing a whip, overturning tables and throwing out greedy merchants who had made the temple a sort of religious strip-mall.

Violence, when used in self-defense, and under the control and direction of moral truth, is a good thing. It's a right thing. It's a needed and, therefore, loving thing.

The problem is that when we lose that eye of the tiger we end up lying to ourselves. We conveniently think that "being nice" is a high virtue. You hear this all the time when someone speaks of a person who committed some awful atrocity. "Ah, but they were so nice," someone opines. Being nice isn't ethical virtue. It's simply a matter of manners. If you pulled up to a four-way stop and Josef Stalin got to the one opposite you right around the same time, maybe before you, and he smiled and waved you through, that would be nice, yes. But it wouldn't change the fact that he was a murderous dictator.

Forgetting this simple thing and losing our edge makes us worse than useless as self-defenders. It will also eviscerate our training by changing the tone of it and adding complexity.

Good self-defense is simple. And brutal. It's not fancy. If it's flashy, it's trashy.

Bad self-defense is often found in schools of Wing Chun where the instructor has, for whatever reason, rejected the reality of mankind; his anthropology is inconsistent with reality. There are schools where Chi-sao is played as some kind of gentle patty-cake, or a hyper-technical game of gotcha. The problem there is anthropological and, therefore, theological. One's theory of man is shown in his martial art training. Bad self-defense training rejects the obvious knowledge that men of violence will be brutal to men and women of peace if they can, and only superior force will stop them.

But a poor philosophy may also lead to those schools of violence where aggression is stressed absent of character. This makes the mistake of thinking that man's problem is, as Albert Mohler once put it, *out there*. This is to say, it's an approach that thinks nothing of the personal necessity *not* to be an instigator, the arsonist, so to speak. A school where a teacher doesn't practice and preach the fundamentals of self-control and respect is a den of aggression, not self-defense. The nobility of martial art is swept away in all that rage, fear, and insecurity that motivates the aggression of lustful men. If you've been appalled, even surprised, to see a martial art "leader" act like a petulant child, or like a thug, you've seen the result of this. A man like Connor McGregor is a fighter, yes, but a martial artist certainly not. On the contrary, a true champion like Georges St. Pierre is rightly respected.

The contrast, or philosophical tension, between the respect and care used in training, especially in a drill like Chi-sao, and the violence that's being trained is only properly understood in this way. Knowledge is knowing the taan-sao and all that; wisdom is knowing *why and when* you'd stick your thumb in another man's eye and smash his head into a wall. Indeed, there's a time and a season for all things under heaven, my friends.

With this said, this author wishes and prays that all Wing Chun men and women be dangerous to no one except the predator. And that it can be said by all who know them that they've never seen them, nor remember an instance where they lost their temper, nor treated another soul disrespectfully. Should we honor athletic talent but dismiss moral virtue? Look at this world and tell me which is the harder to obtain? And tell me which is more important for true life.

So, yes, Chi-sao is technical, yet free and creative. It's violent, yet controlled and respectful. It's aggressive and still respectful, never out of control.

The paradoxes of Chi-sao are due to man's fallen nature - his need of self-discipline *and* aggression in the face of attack. He needs both. If the pendulum swings too far in either direction we have the problems we see around us: hyper traditionalists who turn the art into a museum piece or fight schools who preach practicality as the highest good.

Knowing this keeps it simple and balanced. It reminds us that the real world of violence isn't a match, nor is aggression unethical given the moral context of self-defense. This will inoculate us. It will focus our training and keep us from complexity or over-simplification - from superfluous hand-chasing games or sport dominated practice.

To get Chi-sao right, we must have the correct philosophy of life and man. As always, truth in particulars flow from correct premises.

11

THE GOOD, THE BAD, & THE UGLY

C hi-sao is the genius of Wing Chun. No other fighting method has, as we've pointed out, such a unique laboratory for developing non-contradictory infighting skill/reflexes. While this is certainly true, it's imperative that we properly identify both Wing Chun and its preeminent training drill. Both are inexplicably linked. An improper definition of Wing Chun leads to the debasement, devaluation, or diminishment of Chi-sao. Just as well, if we get the primary idea of Wing Chun down but misidentify Chi-sao's purpose then we've effectively neutered the entire system.

To wit, to call Wing Chun a logic art and science of close-range self-defense is to say that it encompasses the following:

- STRIKING WITH ALL TOOLS (PALMS, fists, fingers, elbows, head, knees, etc.)
    - pushing/pulling
    - footwork and shifting
    - locking and breaking
    - throwing, tripping, etc.
    - even such things as biting

. . .

THIS IS to say that Wing Chun must be a complete infighting system. To be an infighting science as it's alleged but to disregard any single element through which we might inflict pain upon the opponent and, therefore, diminish their effectual capacity, is arbitrary and nonsensical. It's like turning down free money. Or rejecting a cookie. Or going out with the prettiest girl in the world and leaving her at the door awaiting a goodnight kiss. It just doesn't make any sense.

Not only that, but such an infighting method must also include two other things that make it, well, scientific, which is to say in this case, non-contradictory. First, it must include defenses against those same things. Second, it must include within the system a means of training or else the ability is pure potentiality. A fighting art must be actualized. It mustn't stay in the realm of the theoretical. Even the most meat-headed doofus who keeps saying, "let's see that in the Octagon, bro" knows this. He knows it in part, in shadows, and in half-truths, but he knows it.

We claim, of course, that Wing Chun is indeed such a close-range dynamo. We profess and maintain that Wing Chun is unique in the world as a methodology of extreme nastiness that systematically attacks the body's weakest targets, breaks one's balance, slams them into hard stuff, and is generally and comprehensively brilliant. Yes, we say that good Wing Chun is an F5 tornado with forms.

Ah, but not just that. It's Chi-sao that provides the unique training drill to test and develop the ability to put into practice these ridiculously simple, yet brutal, fighting tactics. And it does so in a manner that's progressive and safe. A bunch of dudes who blind each other in training, or rip out each other's throats, or knock kneecaps sideways, aren't going to live very productive lives, right? Ending up blinded and/or crippled on any given Tuesday night due to the harsh realism of one's training makes it hard to hold down productive employment which in turn makes it impossible to pay for classes. Or buy cookies. Or take that pretty girl on a date.

And that's the whole point of it. It must be an integrated package because without a training drill (and its derivatives) to develop trusted reflexes - safely - then we have nothing but a *potential* self-defense system. That's like having an imaginary car. Training is what actualizes the potential of one's forms. Drills are what bring to life the theories and structures trained elsewhere.

That's the *good* of Chi-sao. Many people have asked over the years why our Chi-sao curriculum is different than that of other families. I've always answered that it's not different in the structure. It's just that we do our hearty best to keep the main thing the main thing and that's to remember that the skills we're working on in Chi-sao are going to be deployed in an absolutely terrible situation of extreme violence. That's the thing. It falls out of our head and our skill, if you can call it that, is in never tiring of repeating ourselves.

Some big, nasty dude is coming at you. His aim is to hurt, maim or kill and there's no choice whatsoever. He must be dealt with and there's no avenue of avoidance or escape. There you are and you must answer or else you're in a bad, bad way. There's no faking. There is no maybe anymore. It's time. There's only pure action.

Can you stop him? Can you hurt him? Can you keep him from hurting/killing you? Are you ready? That's pretty much it right there.

Chi-sao must check these boxes. If it doesn't then it's useless. If we think of it as some kind of mystical game of hand-chasing, then it's nothing more than an elaborate and time-consuming lie. Sure you can do it if you want. You can stand there and play fancy patty-cake with a partner and pretend you're a warrior. You can do that and pay a monthly club membership too. That's simply a choice and everyone has that. We aren't denying that. What we're saying is that such a scheme won't work under the type of pressure we just described.

And this brings us to the *bad*.

Bad Chi-sao is the stuff you see in those schools of Wing Chun that have jettisoned the truth about combat. Yeah, they've made minor things the main thing. I've heard of schools that don't allow pushing, head strikes, or grabbing and kicking in Chi-sao. They've made it a gentlemanly game more appropriate to tea and crumpets than fighting. You know what I'm talking about. They're all formal and wet their pants if someone's bong-sao isn't pristine. The emphasis is on everything *but* the control and destruction of the enemy's fighting ability. These deluded fellows have made Wing Chun into a museum piece. They're like a man running into a battle-field to lecture the combatants about their crude technique. They've been defeated by the success of civilization wherein it hasn't crossed their minds that someone in this fallen world might, gasp, actually try and hurt them.

This is the source of the bad Wing Chun and you see it in their Chi-sao. No one's moving. No one's trying to take the other fella's balance. It's so formalized that the idea of *scientifically and safely cheating* is anathema. They're like someone who has a tank that's painted with rainbows and flowers that's parked in a garden. They've tried to make a war machine into a rose forgetting that Wing Chun is beautiful precisely because it's so efficient at its job. Indeed, bringing order to the ugly chaos of self-defense, of real-world violence in all its tyranny, is itself a thing of beauty.

So, what's the *ugly?* Ugly is the thing it does to the rest of the system. The irrational dichotomy that's created when we say that Wing Chun is, in fact, the sort of thing we've said, but that Chi-sao is trained illogically is ugly indeed. It eviscerates the method. It renders it useless by way of leaving it purely in the realm of theory and potential. It creates sloppiness where there should be consum-mate skill. The fine-tuned fighting machine that good Chi-sao develops is a professional who looks to others as someone who merely - almost magically - gets people by the head, face, eyes and throat, and steals their balance. All at once.. The movements of attack and defense are so integrated as to be invisible to all but the trained eye. The footwork and shifting operating in unison with the compact and springy hands allow the Wing Chun professional to do all this aforementioned violence in such a way as to seem almost natural. But it's not natural at all, but the product of years of training - specifically in Chi-sao.

Bad Chi-sao that's misdirected either through the tyranny of hyper-traditionalists or the anarchy of men without discipline and philosophy, achieve only the severing of theory and practice. And that, my friends, is ugly in the way putting a camper on a your pickup truck is. Okay...maybe not that ugly. But really, really ugly.

12

WAY OF NO WAY...OR SOMETHING LIKE THAT

I generally get along with all sorts of people. I'm a people person, in fact. Of course, there's that rather odd fact that I also hit people a lot too but that's usually with a padded fist. And it's consensual, you know. I mean, it's sparring. It's not like I'm whacking people upside the head and taking their wallet and then calling myself a people person.

But that's just the thing. It's called context and everyone gets that. In other words, people understand that context is king. That's an everyday, rubber hits the road sort of reasoning and if we can't do that then we aren't adulting well at all. A dude that doesn't understand the difference between a fire truck running red lights and him doing it on the way to the market isn't going to keep his license very long.

You may even call such a thing *common sense* and I've no objection to that. As we've already mentioned, there's actually a philosophy from a few hundred years ago called *Scottish Common-Sense Realism* that taught that Scottish people were much more logical than, say, the cheese-eating French.

Just kidding.

In all seriousness, though, the idea of saying one is using

"common sense" is actually rather deep philosophy. There are quite a few integrations to make in order to arrive at such a place. You see, a guy who says he uses common sense is a guy who's saying that reality is knowable, can be understood rightly by man's faculty of reason, and that it's a virtue to abide by logic. You might even call such a man a philosopher who ascribes to the "correspondence view" of truth, which is to say that he believes what is true is that which corresponds to reality.

Before you get bored and flip the page, trust me, more jokes are coming. Maybe even a reference to an evil ex or something like that. You know, something we can all relate to. Until then suffice it to say that our fictional common sense dude is quite the philosopher. He's a philosopher of *fact*. He's got his feet firmly planted in reality because...and here's the big point...his whole focus is reality.

Truth is that which is real. Reality simply doesn't care about whether or not we agree with it and life is that simple. Vanity is what makes life complicated. It's really not too hard to understand that we live in a world of physical and moral laws and those laws are, if you will, that which is rightly referred to as reality. Stupid men are vain men. Vanity makes us stupid because it attempts to elevate us over against reality and every time reality is challenged by man, reality is undefeated.

Let's be clear about something important. A stupid man and an uneducated one aren't the same thing, although sometimes they cross paths. The uneducated man isn't necessarily stupid - at least not in the context we care about here. A doofus who couldn't put together a coherent argument about the facts of life to, well, save his life, isn't exactly stupid in the way we mean. He respects the laws of reality just like other men. He looks both ways before he crosses the street. He doesn't pick fights he knows he'll lose. He's not educated but he's not self-destructive because he knows that reality is greater than he is.

A stupid man, though, is a fellow who flaunts common sense laws of reality as a regular rule. These often charming folks are all over the place these days. They don't dare challenge some of reality's laws but routinely ignore others. Gravity? Not gonna mess with that one. Physical laws, when broken, have rather immediate consequences so most of us don't bother picking fights. Sure, there are always lovable knuckleheads called daredevils who get too close to the cliff's edge, but even there we see respect. After all, the daredevil stakes their acclaim on the very fact that they're literally flirting with danger. So, you see, there's still respect.

Moral laws, though as real as physical laws, and we'd argue that they're more real but that's another subject for another book, don't give as immediate a smack down to violators. For that reason and that one alone we skip along the edge. That's why the further a person or institution gets from the consequences of their actions, the more foolish they become. For example, which group of people, In general, are more realistic? This is to ask which is more immediately restrained by the consequences of their ideas? Firemen or politicians? An English major or a plumber? An economics professor or a small business owner? A Navy SEAL or a philosophy professor?

We all know this. It's common sense, right? A person or business that's got "skin in the game" is more trustworthy than any person or institution that's far removed from bad ideas. And this is precisely why every culture struggles with utter nonsense as it grows wealthier. The human tendency is to try and avoid accountability. We all know that. Just go spend some time with young children. You'll never hear a parent saying, "Now, Tommy, you didn't need to take responsibility for that. It wasn't your fault. I know you like Mary and wish she had turned her homework in too but it's not your fault that she didn't listen to you."

And this leads us to the concept of unity and diversity. It leads us to the heavily abused Bruce Lee quote, "have no way as way."

Many people head-hunt in Wing Chun and eschew the body as a prime target. Watch how Sifu Tony uses lop-sao with a short hook to the body.

When using Lop-sao, the enemy gets yanked off balance. This makes attacking the head a difficult thing in many cases... especially if, as shown here, the opponent rides the momentum and moves their head. Now, granted, that's not the normal Wing Chun response but that's exactly what we have to be ready for. Sifu Tony is. Not being "chained" to a wooden definition of the art, he fires a short punch to my body. Of course, we all know that in reality he'd break his hand on my rock-hard abs but we're just practicing here. Carry on.

THE PROBLEM IS that some hacks have gotten hold of it. They've taken it to mean something outside the realm of common sense. And it's to this that we say that Chi-sao is a means of producing skill at surviving an unavoidable, close-range attack. Everything else that we might get from the drill is subordinate to this primary thing. If at a point in our lives/training we wish to focus on some auxiliary thing that's certainly our right. But the thing we must not do is violate the core tenet of Wing Chun's Chi-sao, which is combat survival.

Once we have that down firmly in our minds we're free to explore the wonderful diversity of benefits in the drill. It's fun. It's completely unique! There's nothing else like it. It's a chess match like no other. It gives the Wing Chun student a chance to "test" their knowledge with one another and all that. Yeah. But that's like getting married because there's a reason to buy a bigger bed. That's totally missing the point and unless we keep the main point fixed in our minds we'll either turn Chi-sao into something it's not (a kind of Wing Chun duel) or jettison the drill altogether.

Another example of not being bound by a hyper-traditional approach. Sifu Tony executes a Paak-Da, but instead of staying in a Wing Chun orientated position, I slip to the outside and get ready to counter.

In this case, Sifu Tony picks up my hook to the body by shifting back (facing) and using a Gaun-sao and hit. Remember: use Wing Chun; don't be used by it. Oh, and just like with the rock-hard abs, we all know that the author is so fast that he would have slipped, gone home, made dinner, done some chores, taken a shower, and still had time to get back to throw the hook. I'm just slowing down for the photos. Just saying.

FOR EXAMPLE, a lot of us like to "play" at it. We like rolling and doing some "feisty" attacks with one another. Others prefer to keep it like a tai-chi exercise with a partner. Every Wing Chun family has their own way of doing it - that is, there's a stylistic difference in how the principles are applied. Watch Ip Ching roll and he's got almost no discernible pattern. Other families stay in a very distinctive format, arms moving back and forth, left to right, right to left. Ip Ching's Chi-sao was left-to-right as well as forward-backward. In other words, there was no predictable pattern to it because at his level he was "jamming"...he was like Hendrix or Clapton. Ip Ching's Chi-sao was "no way as way" due to his lifetime of devotion to the craft.

But what happens when we forget the lifetime devotion part? Then we get "no way as way" meaning incompetence rather than mastery, that's what.

You see, here in America especially, we have this terrible

tendency to think too highly of ourselves. We seek shortcuts. We want everything yesterday. And to do that we have to get rid of the reality of testing. So, yes, we can and should "play at it" and have fun. There's no sin in that. But we must resist the temptation to fall asleep in all that and remember what it is we're doing this for.

13

THE FLAT SQUIRREL SYNDROME

Sifu Tony Massengill isn't just a master of Wing Chun. He's certainly that. And, no, he's not the president and/or client of the *Hairclub For Men* in case you're wondering. What he is is an absolute expert in the fine art of coming up with pithy ways of stating complex things.

Without further delay, the *flat squirrel syndrome,* as he calls it, is the act of standing indecisively in the middle of the road when there's trouble headed your way. That's exactly how you get run over, right? If the poor fella simply darted right or left all would be fine. But panic hits and it can't make up its mind. Well, violence is quite like this in case you were wondering where we're going. Hesitation and indecisiveness are deadly.

Sifu Tony, from a career in law enforcement and fire/rescue, told me once that lots of people died in fires because they wasted critical seconds deciding the best exit instead of running to ANY exit. They stood there too long, inhaling that burning smoke, looking for the perfect course of action. Well, as Patton said in that perfectly Patton-esque way of his, a brutal and swift plan executed right now beats the perfect one *next week.*

Living in a fallen world, we're always shocked by how fast time goes, aren't we? We always like to think we have more time and that's usually one of the chief laments of someone when they face death. "I thought I'd have more time," they say in that weakened voice full of regret and resignation as the inevitable closes in. Well, violence shatters that whole sad self-sale of procrastination and lethargy. It's here and we must act. There's literally no time. A dying man and a man under assault learn, at last, to appreciate the inestimable value of time.

For this reason I make no apologies for being blunt. I know...it's a quality in life that some people care less for than a rainy weekend. That's okay. I've learned over the years that I don't care much for the type of folks that prefer the soft blanket of half-truths and lies over the often chilly directness of truth. I've struggled with that. Aren't we supposed to love everyone and all that? Yes, we are. But love without truth isn't really love and when someone asks that we compromise a moral standard, or the truth itself, then that's the time to "not be nice" (to borrow that great line from Dalton).

Wing Chun is a system of self-defense. And self-defense is the art and science of keeping oneself as safe as possible in the event of unavoidable violence. And when violence is unavoidable one has the moral right to fight. Not merely that, but one *should* fight. And one should fight to survive! Period. The consequences of losing (and we aren't talking about a match but an honest to goodness assault) are horrific.

This definition precludes, of course, just getting into a fight over some minor, or petty, provocation. And they're all petty provocations. A real martial art gets this right...he differentiates between competition and honest-to-goodness violence; he doesn't blur the line because to do so is immoral. To conflate competition with the ugliness that is tyrannical violence is a special kind of folly. Sporting competition is a noble thing; the competitors train hard to win a prize within the confines of civilized rules. The fact that these endeavors are considered brutish or cruel by some isn't the point. Where there are rules imposed by civilization, and the freedom to choose to compete, there is generally honor along with it. That's not the case in self-defense. Self-defense, seen logically, is about the worst. It's about barbarism and, therefore, a contest of survival and freedom. The intended victim is fighting not to be dehumanized because assaults, murders and rapes are precisely that: acts of dehumanization. For that reason, any spirited defense is an act of humanity and love.

If we lose this distinction we surrender the motive power of martial art. And this is certainly why a martial art that fails to teach the codes of honor, specifically self-control and respect for all, ends up losing the battle before it begins. Why? Because it's precisely the loss of self-control and respect for others that leads to conflict and violence in the first place. If literally everyone controlled themselves and treated others as they themselves want to be treated, never as a means to an end, I wouldn't have a job. A martial art school, therefore, is a profoundly moral place. In a world that starts its moral reasoning with *personal feelings*, this often strikes people as odd. Nevertheless, moral law is the foundation of martial art. To jettison moral law and the Royal Commandments as the foundation of martial art leads us to wholesale confusion. It leads to the absurdities we see everyday. It's like calling Jack-the-Ripper merely a poor surgeon. Without self-control and respect at the core, we aren't a member of a martial art school, we're in a gang.

A martial art is the logical outworking of the fact that we live in a fallen world where violence exists. It (martial art) must exist or else all men will be slaves.

This said, the best defense is a good offense and the best offense is a counterattack because it (countering) includes the defense with the offense. The counterattack integrates offense and defense so that there's no contradiction. That's the whole idea behind the *Jeet*. It's the truth of this concept applied. To intercept an attack with a structurally superior attack is the whole idea. Simultaneous attack and defense, *lin siu daai da,* literally is Wing Chun. Wing Chun is, therefore, a systematic of aggressive defense. Without the systematic we have a wild and undisciplined reply that may or may not be effective. Granted, any violent response to violence is better, morally as well as tactically, than none, but the goal of scientific training is to diminish the risk of injury as much as possible. This is why Wing Chun is a system of fistic logic. This is what it means to say *Wing Chun Kuen Hok* - or, Wing Chun fist (combat) science. Better still is *Wing Chun Sum Fat*, which is to say Wing Chun heart (Sum) law (Fat).

The flat squirrel is one that doesn't keep the main thing the main thing. In Wing Chun we hear the word simplicity a lot and yet we don't have people define it in practice. Simplicity in self-defense is (assuming that escape and avoidance are off the table) the act of rendering your attacker(s), as expeditiously as possible, incapable of continuing their threat. Every action and tactic applied has this goal in mind and is graded by this standard. This is why, for example, we attack the head, neck, and throat of the enemy with the logical structure developed by Wing Chun training. Or the groin or knees. And we do it with logical structure that's non-contradictory and complete emotional commitment.

One way to end up a flat squirrel that you may not have thought about is through a lack of moral commitment to hurting your enemy. Yeah, that's right. Really hurting him. You see, there's an old saying... something about mean often prevails over good when good isn't mean. Real violence is going to severely test one's emotional readiness, not just our physical reflexes. It's going to require the courage to literally fight back by attacking an enemy with bad intentions. A half-hearted response with great technique is a terrible response. One's morale must be high. The self-defender must have given themselves the green-light ahead of time in order to function under the stress of combat since there's no time to think anyway.

Kaitlyn shows the fruit of both good technical training (she attacks the middle I left open in trying to grab her) and proper emotional readiness for the reality of unavoidable violence. If she isn't truly ready on both counts - technically and emotionally - she'll be a victim.

This is what Napoleon meant when he said that in war the moral is to the physical as three is to one.

The attacker often has this significant advantage. He's already decided that he'll use violence to achieve a value. The decision has already been made and all he needs are the victim and opportunity to both align. This is what makes the attacker a formidable foe, despite having, in very many cases, no formal training in the arts of combat. He's all in. He's completely unimpaired by moral confusion or vacillation. The flat squirrel is, therefore, the trained person who, for whatever reason, hasn't committed to the fight.

The reason for this is often social conventions and the vanity inspired by them. In others words, it's a theological problem stemming from our misapprehension of the nature of man.

It's vanity to think that human beings are morally good. Being "nice" is conforming to social conventions; being righteous is being conformed to God's moral law.

I've had legalistic nitpickers criticize my teaching methods in the past. One woman was greatly perturbed that while teaching her teenage daughter how not to be raped I mentioned the word "balls"... as in, "kick him in the balls." She insisted that there was no need for that kind of language. Oh, and she carried on with something like, "I don't have my children in a bubble or anything...". Yes, she does. A bubble of smoke and vanity.

When I explained that teaching technique alone while eschewing the emotional ferocity to use that technique is like giving someone a gun without bullets, she wasn't convinced. She was intent upon living in a make-believe world where Cain never killed Abel, in a world of sunshine and rainbows and nice things. And unicorns. The plain fact is that mankind is evil. No other fact of history is more easily proven than man's inhumanity toward those who get in his way.

Another woman didn't understand why we were swinging pool noodles at the heads of children so they'd learn to slip, duck and cover. When I said that the noodles were better than, say, actual fists, she grew even more irritated. And incidentally, when I say she didn't understand, let's not take that to infer that she humbly sought guidance and clarity. On the contrary, though she'd admittedly never been in a fight in her life, she stridently informed me that she thought it was all unnecessary. She was convinced that the problem of violence could be solved in a much nicer way than I was teaching it.

Sigh.

Why swing soft objects at children in the attempt to teach them reflexes - you know, good muscle memory - for when someone really swings at them? Good grief! Our anthropology is severely flawed when we come to the conclusion that swinging pool noodles is too aggressive. That's what we mean by calling such cultural rubbish vanity. It's vanity indeed. It's the soft pillow of deceit that we fall asleep upon, convinced that because we live with nice things that means we're nice. Everything is about being nice, not moral, and the thought that hand-to-hand combat can't be conducted quietly and, yes, nicely, is just all too much. *"Oh, well, I never!!"*

It's also false morality. It's the belief that if I don't use certain words and do certain things, then I'm morally pure. This ignores the problem that the Lord explains so wonderfully well in Jeremiah 17:9. The heart is, indeed, deceptively wicked and man's evil is at its worst when hidden under the veneer of *nice*. Being nice is a cultural virtue but not always a moral virtue. A man or woman of good moral character will often be considered nice, but a nice person isn't necessarily moral. The point not to miss is, trust me, that being a victim of assault, rape, or murder, because you were unprepared for reality because you were too busy being nice, isn't a virtue at all.

One of the benefits of Wing Chun's Chi-sao training is that the student learns to attack and defend simultaneously at close-quarter clinching/grappling range. Sifu Tony always says that in real fights we hit people with things and things with people . It's easier to do this against enemy's who haven't been trained in the non-contradictory science of in-fighting. In this case, after Devin pulled his head back to avoid a strike, I was able to seize the initiative and "help him along."

This is the sort of nonsense that gets people killed. Teaching martial arts in America where there's a Starbucks every 20 feet is sometimes like trying to teach dogs to read. We've been educated to think that morality is whatever makes me feel good. We've been taught, through so much propaganda, that feelings are tools of cognition. We convince ourselves that because we've developed a "consumer" culture that we literally have power over reality. But we can't treat violence like Starbucks or McDonalds. We can't "have it our way" because there's a vast difference between an unavoidable attack and a coffee.

There are a great many things wrong with modern America. One of the most dangerous is that material wealth has allowed a generation to think that what they feel about the world *is the world*. Reality doesn't care about one's feelings anymore than gravity gives two hoots *why* a man is falling. He's falling and that's all there is to it. Just as well, if someone is trying to kill you you must understand that he has the advantage of ferocity if you're irresolute. Fighting back with extreme hatred of evil is good. Being morally ambivalent is literally evil because the only common ground between good and evil is the battleground. There's a clear reason why Chamberlain is considered a rube and a coward and Churchill a hero. And it's always evil to play god over another human being, to deny them their right to disagree, and to live their life with the same freedom we have.

Evil and violence flourish in any era or place where bad men don't fear good ones. Yes, it's that simple. Fighting is dirty business but it's not inherently immoral. Violence in defense is morally good. The whole thing comes down to the context. So, please, don't fall prey to the lie, to the con, to the vain masquerade that we live in a world of good people. They aren't good. You aren't good. I'm not good. If we define that word - good - carefully we get at the root of it. If good means nice then, yeah, I suppose we have millions and millions of nice people out there. But if we define it as morally righteous, then that's another thing altogether.

The reality is that we're violent and bossy and prone to using others as a means to an end. We either do that directly if we have the power, or through some kind of outsourced mechanism. HOA boards, lawyers, politicians, lobbyists...all of that. What are they but attempts to control others? Conflict is inevitable so long as any man thinks himself to be the final arbiter of right and wrong, a moral law unto himself. A true martial artist understands this foundational theological/philosophical flaw as the source of violence and, therefore, swears to abide by the correct code.

What is that exactly? He/she swears to respect all neighbors and never, under any circumstances, directly or through a proxy, abridge the God-given liberty, of both life and property, of anyone. He/she also takes the responsibility to train in order to meet aggression with the science of self-defense. In doing so, they realize that they too are a member of this fallen human race, so they cherish and submit to the moral code lest they be what they're training to defend against in the first place. The martial artist is a man or woman of the utmost realism, seeing themselves and the world around them rightly.

Like Ip Man before us, who lived in a violent world of war and oppression (chiefly, invasion by Imperial Japan and sure persecution and maybe death under Maoist commies), we remain at peace with all insofar as it depends on us, but always ready for defense.

So, moral philosophy and righteousness are not abstract things. They're as much a part of good martial art as any technique and, in fact, more important, because a defender who doesn't understand them is likely to end up as the flat squirrel. Even more, the "martial artist" who denies this is the very predator against whom self-defense is needed. Logical moral philosophy is the pure gasoline that powers the engine of our technique.

14

TESTING THE LOGIC OF WING CHUN - OR, HOW WE KNOW WE AREN'T FULL OF STUFF

I n the title of this chapter, we use the word logic instead of the popular word science. As it goes, the latter is a much-abused thing these days and it's been bandied about with such alarming recklessness to have lost its honor. Science has become, in our brain-dead age of specialists and their beloved central planning, whatever the *experts* say it is. We must ignore, of course, that this very thought runs afoul of the laws of logic - specifically, the fallacy of appeal to authority. Truth is truth, after all and isn't swayed because an expert said otherwise.

Do we need to remind ourselves that the Titanic was steered unceremoniously into that iceberg by experts? Even a blithering idiot could have warned a man that running a ship full speed ahead, in the dark, through the semi-frozen waters of the North Atlantic in April, was as unsound as driving with one's eyes closed. Or borrowing money from the mob. Or telling your wife that your ex-girlfriend is looking pretty good on Instagram.

But that's the thing at hand. Common sense, as Mark Twain reportedly opined, ain't so common. The obvious dies a ruthless and self-inflicted death every day because desire overrules the obvious right before our eyes. And this is the issue with modern use of science. It simply can't be scientific if it's illogical.

One day when I was a young man I went to the mall with a friend. We had to go to a store, long gone now, called *Caldors*. It was a massive department store that sold nearly everything in the age before Wal-Mart. In this case, he needed something for his car... maybe an oil filter...maybe a new transmission. I forget which. You could also pick up a nice pair of jeans on sale too.

Anyway, in that dark age before Amazon and the internet, there we were walking along when I saw her. She was in a store called *Record Town* looking at these new and exotic things called CDs. Since it was the 80's, as you may have guessed, she had an enormous hairstyle piled up and out, blond, and bold. If there was an earthquake and the building collapsed, you would have been able to pull survivors from all that hair. Anyway, all that blonde-ness caught my attention. Then the rest of her did.

Don't judge me. I was 19.

She had her back to me. She wore a skirt. A tight one. I think she had a top on. She must have but I don't remember that. To this day all I remember was the hair and the skirt.

I stopped in my tracks and my buddy and I regarded the splendid scene for a long moment. Not being one to dither around, I walked in and said hello.

"Can I help you?" I asked.

She looked at me with evident puzzlement because I was wearing a shirt and shorts (we'd been playing basketball earlier in the day).

I laughed at her expression and said, "No, I don't work here. But I'd really like to help you."

She laughed probably because I was laughing. Being goofy and looking stupid was (is) my way of being charming in the absence, truth be told, of any real charm.

"No..." she said, "I think I'm fine."

"Yes," I replied, "you certainly are that."

Such a bad joke, I know. But coupled with my dumb grin she couldn't fight a laugh.

"So, listen, me and that ugly friend of mine out there in the hall have to go get a part for his car. Could I interest you in a cup of coffee or something afterward? We can talk about CD's, music, car parts, or anything else your heart desires."

Okay...okay, as Hugh Grantish good as all that was, she actually said no.

Seriously.

Apparently, it's hard to be handsome and charming when you're wearing a t-shirt and shorts.

That must have been it. Momma always said I was handsome.

Anyway, we went on to Caldors, got whatever it was we went there for, and then passed her again on the way back. I tried again... accusing her of following me. This time the jokes worked and I convinced her to get a quick bite at the food court. (This whole story is soooo very 80's!)

Where am I going with all this? Simple. After talking with her for a bit it was quite evident that we had virtually nothing in common. And that she may have been, shall we say, a rather tempestuous beauty. In other words, smart Jason would have recognized this and moved on. Dumb Jason, made so by virtue of the girl's beauty and no longer thinking straight, forged ahead.

In case you can't see the obvious coming, there's a mushroom cloud where that relationship used to be.

But seriously, it's just a funny and all too common example of ways, great and small, that we lose sight of the main thing. Our desires, egos, lusts, passions, fears, insecurities...they can and do cloud our faculties of reason. It literally happens to every single person. None of us are immune. If a boxer were to say that he doesn't ever worry about dropping his hands because it can't happen to him, or if a gun instructor professed that he never worries about an accidental discharge, we'd hear the hubris warning bells loud and clear. It's the same with the so-called experts of late. *Trust me, I'm an expert and can't be wrong* are some of the scariest words in any language.

Thus, I'm not using the word science because, as mentioned, it's been rather divorced from logic lately and that's a dangerous thing. Especially for something as important as self-defense. After all, it's your life on the line. Moreover, in that vein, because this subject is so critical, and even your humble and charming author has a past in which he's been blind to a blunder, we humbly present this material to the scrutiny of logic.

In other words, we're concerned with the exigent question of "what if I'm wrong?" So, a little laborious though it might be, and in the way of intellectual honesty, we want to bow before that altar of truth that all men must since we aren't, nor can be, truth itself. My personal credentials in Wing Chun, self-defense, Jeet Kune Do, writing, and picking up pretty girls at the mall (spectacularly impressive though that last thing was), are all beside the point when it comes to the truth claim that Wing Chun is the most logical close-range self-defense system available to men and women. It may be. Or maybe it's not. Reality has the last word and as I believe any writer-teacher-authority ought to do in these dark days of anti-philosophy and brain-dead worship of credentials, I willingly submit to the laws of logic.

Naturally, I think this material is correct or else I wouldn't be writing it. Plus, I've personally used it for my own defense in the past. Yes, that's true, but lots of variables go into something like that and this isn't an appeal to subjectivity. After all, you might be thinking that the fights I prevailed in are tainted. Perhaps my opponents were awful. They could've been drunken losers who would've lost a fight to a heavy bag. Or I could be lying. So, it's always a question. How do we know we can trust this stuff? How do we know... truly know, that this is gonna work?

How do we arrive at the truth of the matter? How can we have reasonable certainty that we aren't missing the mark? How can we be sure that the beautiful blond or the awesome Wing Chun we're smitten with isn't going to break our hearts (or heads) someday in the future? Alas, that's the big question we ought all to take seriously. It's also important to remember that fighting is a clash of speed and power. A powerful athlete may very well get away with illogical technique and tactics by virtue of the simple fact that he was stronger than his enemy. But physical attributes are fickle and must not be relied on as a continued source of success. What if we run into someone strong or fast enough to nullify our advantages? A logical combat systematic must assume that the enemy is slower and weaker.

To that end, our approach is twofold.

First is the systematic presentation of the theory of Wing Chun and self-defense. Next is the application of the laws of logic over on top of it. In other words, *philosophy and logic*. Logic can't give us the content of truth. But by virtue of the laws of contradiction it can tell us *what can't be true*. To arrive at a contradiction is to discover an error. Certainly there's nothing wrong with being wrong but there's a lot wrong with deliberately staying wrong. To err is human, right? I'd offer that to be wrong is evidence that we're human but to stay wrong is evidence that we're either indifferent to truth or , much worse, flat-out immoral.

Theoretical philosophy provides the content of truth. Logic acts as its governor. If it's contradictory it can't be true. That's the gist of logic right there. Logic can't tell us what is true, but it absolutely tells us what can't be true. And since we're all prone to error, we should cheerfully throw all our truth claims in that great sieve of logic to see what's left. An illogical philosophy is a contradiction in terms.

What we're doing therefore is presenting the Wing Chun theory of self-defense and checking our math with logic. Simple. The insistence upon carefully defining the terms - especially self-defense (which is the act of keeping oneself as safe as possible in the event of unavoidable violence) - *literally is the practice of logic*!

The first sign that error has crept in is that we stop reducing our theories back to the fundamentals. Truth-claims like Wing Chun (and every other discipline of action too) must be, in its systematic, internally consistent with itself, and externally consistent with the facts of reality. Any contradiction internally or externally isn't a mere fly in the ointment but cyanide on your sandwich.

The other reason for an approach like this is that we're planted in an age of unprecedented irrationality which has impacted all of us.

Our educational processes intentionally suppress the ability to think in *categories*. This is the greatest threat to freedom, which makes it, indubitably, a self-defense issue. A person who can't think logically is in grave danger as he navigates a world of lies. It's impossible to retain one's liberty if easily duped.

No one would send in a dolt or bonehead to buy a car for them. A salesman would run roughshod all over them and you'd end up driving a 20 year-old car in a color you hate for more than you'd pay for a mortgage. On a subject so small as that we know the truth. An intellectually unprepared fellow is in danger of being duped. That's just the way it is. Well, it's so much worse in real life than shopping for a car. The unphilosophical man or woman is literally making life or death decisions about truth and reality everyday. Worse than that, our so-called scientific culture brings us to the dessert buffet of emotions and calls that a good diet. The veggies of sound logic are nowhere to be seen.

Let me show you how bad it is.

The next time someone mentions how much they hate the president or some politician, casually ask them what their theory of government is. They'll blink at you like you just asked your dog to recite a poem. And it's not entirely their fault because, as we said, the education methodology deliberately avoids teaching in systematics and categories. To do so requires the logic of identification. To define a category is to bring one's attention to the nature and identity of a thing. The first step in pushing propaganda is to eviscerate the ability to define the category in question.

WHAT IS GOVERNMENT FOR? *What is its nature and goal?*

YOU SEE, the moment we ask such a question(s) people will respond intellectually the way an out of shape dude will if you take him for a run. All of a sudden they get frustrated because their thoughts are jumbled. The lack of systematics causes them to run into the law of contradiction, like a blindfolded man smacking headfirst into walls, looking feverishly for the door. And that's the thing. We can't make sense out of what makes no sense - which is to say that what's contradictory can't be made rational. A man can believe whatever he wants but he can't make reality bend to his will.

This is why, of course, science must be logical. The disciplines of logic and science are necessary for man's mind to conform to the facts of reality. Logic is the art of non-contradictory identification of the facts of reality. Logic is the discipline of thinking well. Knowing how to live well...that is, to apply "common sense" to everyday things, is to use wisdom. In other words, wisdom is knowing how to live well. Knowing what a thing is doesn't automatically mean we know what to do with it. Wisdom is, therefore, the ability to think with common sense realism about the categories of life. The inability to think categorically is a philosophical/theological error that leads to the disarray and bedlam we see overtaking America.

To live well, men and women must act in truth. To do this we must think logically. And to do this, because reality is diverse, we must understand philosophical categories so we have the ability to grasp the context of an event or thing. And to understand these categories we must take the time to arrive at non-contradictory foundations because all evaluations of facts, all theories of action, proceed from a premise or foundation. All the dissension we see in politics are downstream of this issue. Arguments and strife proceed from *lack of truth*. There can never be real peace where there isn't truth and there's no truth where we find flawed premises. All reasoning is based upon philosophical foundations and if these first principles are flawed we may here and there run into practicality, but in the end we smash headlong into the impenetrable walls of contradiction.

LET's apply this to Wing Chun, shall we?

First, what is it? It's a logical system of self-defense. What's self-defense? It's the discipline of keeping oneself as safe as possible in the event of unavoidable violence. If it's avoidable, it's not self-defense. The law against contradiction asserts itself here...with a vengeance. Self-defense is the morally correct use of violence to protect oneself from imminent loss of life, safety, property, or liberty. Using violence in any other instance is not technically self-defense, but something else, and that change of context alters the principles, purpose, mechanics and tactics of the thing. Like target practice is different from self-defense shooting, so it is with Wing Chun. It's reality that makes demands on Wing Chun (or any other method) and not the other way around. Thus, to arrive at truth insofar as Wing Chun is concerned it must conform to the logical reality of the aforementioned definition.

The *category of self-defense supersedes the discipline of Wing Chun.*

The root of every mistake in Wing Chun is because we drop the full context. Indeed, we might go so far as to say that all mistakes in life can be reduced to categorical context-dropping. All truth is absolute within its context. And nothing is a context unto itself except God. This was painfully evident during our recent mash-ups over COVID restrictions and social policy.

Defenders of lockdowns and all that routinely retreated to screaming "science" at anyone who questioned a policy like mask-wearing or closures. But this was like me yelling "self-defense" anytime someone questions why we do Chi-sao a certain way. They were confusing the application within a category with the category itself. The principles of scientifically identifying the fact of the virus did not logically lead to the applications of economic, social and political actions. In fact, those actions, as I'm doing here, need to be *logically reduced* back to their foundation.

Those actions/policies may or may not have been logical. That's not the point at hand. What's imperative to understand is that it was the philosophical context dropping that caused all the chaos. Knowing one thing certainly doesn't mean we know all the things related to it with equal certainty. In our age of hyper-specialization it's important that we don't commit the fallacy of appeal to authority when considering a subject.

For instance, those who pushed for radical lockdowns in the face of the virus confused scientific certainty over the *fact of the virus* with ethical, political and financial reactions to the fact. In other words, the brute fact of COVID-19 didn't lead necessarily to other facts. That's why we're calling it a brute fact. What happened, and we all lived through this, was that if someone questioned the wisdom of school-closures, they were branded as "anti-science." This was hardly a logical response and we bring it up because it's instructive to our point at hand. It shows how easily we can lose our way.

Again: knowing one thing for certain does not mean we know the affiliate issues with the same clarity.

To that end, we know that unwarranted aggression is morally wrong. What to do about it brings us to the subject (category) of self-defense. If we use Wing Chun for self-defense, it's self-defense that's the goal. Wing Chun is an assistant, not the goal itself. This sweeps away lots of debris blocking our path. Much trouble comes from the context dropping of thinking Wing Chun is the goal itself.

A WING CHUN trainee that devotes countless hours to Chi-sao and forms but neglects physical conditioning and tactical training may very well discover that he's dropped the context of self-defense. We see the problem when people are more concerned with auxiliary points such as lineage over against combat effectiveness. This is putting the minor thing in charge of the major theme. It's a philosophical context drop.

This is an issue, by the way, that's attracted some great minds. Socrates, for example, was rather interested in why men often chose the wrong thing. They become convinced, illogically, that a certain course of action will make them happy.

You see, there's a psychological element to all of this, which is why we need to be careful and check our math (logic) for contradictions. The important thing is to make sure we don't context drop and end up wasting precious resources (time) on the wrong thing.

A lot of students have gotten into BJJ over the years because they heard it was a very effective self-defense system. They didn't want to waste their time training in something that wouldn't work under pressure. Seeing that most MMA fighters train in BJJ, they figured it was a safe bet.

But many ended up getting sucked into the competition feedback loop of modern BJJ. It's the same thing with most boxing gyms too. The emphasis isn't on the "martial" aspect of the discipline anymore...it's all about competition and this shift of focus comes with consequences. Contradictions abound.

Most people don't know that modern and classical boxing differ immensely. If they think about it they assume the differences are due to advances in application ability rather than a drop of context. Old-school boxers were taught mainly in the bare knuckle version of the art. It was the sweet science of self-defense first, and a competition method second. Sparring with protective equipment was a part of training and subordinate to the goal of bare knuckle fighting. Now, sparring literally *is boxing* in most gyms. In the 19th century, the professors forbid their pupils from throwing punches specific to the use of the mufflers (what they called boxing gloves back then). They insisted on good technique like the use of the vertical fist.

Today, though, boxers wrap their hands and then put on gloves. That's not the reality of street-defense and broken hands are a true danger to the modern boxer. Not only that but because of the glove, the knowledge of straight hitting has all but disappeared. Worse still, depending on how you look at it (it's a plus for those of us who know the truth), virtually no one realizes how much damage a straight punch does to the middle of the face.

BJJ has the same problem. By focusing entirely on sport application, training practices have emphasized tactics and techniques that are in some cases antithetical to real combat and in others less than optimal.

This is all to say that there's no "perfect and true" martial art because we're trying to solve the problem of self-defense. And though we know some things comprehensively (such as the moral foundation of self-defense) we don't know with equal comprehensiveness all the derivative points. We know that violent altercations may be on uneven/unsafe footing but we aren't certain exactly where this will be. In fact, we may find that our theatre of defense is actually on good footing. That's certainly possible. And we know that attacks to the eyes and groin are more efficacious than those to harder targets, we don't know precisely that those attacks will absolutely debilitate the enemy.

We're dealing with probabilities in these cases.

That's what all the debating is about.

You see, we aren't saying in any way that a boxer or an MMA fighter *can't* defend themselves. What we're talking about is logical conformity to the facts as we know them. A crazed man who goes "ape" (as we used to say when I was a kid) may find good success in his defense by virtue of being wild and unpredictable. I know of a wrestler who shot in and did a double leg against a fella. The bad guy smacked his melon on the ground as a result and was KO'd. Fight over. Did I mention that the bad guy had a bat? You see? I wouldn't normally think a takedown against a guy with a bat is the best idea but it worked there.

A few years later the same wrestler used the very same takedown (he was very good at it) against an unarmed assailant. This time he ended up breaking his patella - smashing it into several horrifically painful pieces. The guy with the bat attacked him when they were on grass but the second time he was on cement.

And therein was the contradiction. Wrestling is a fine discipline but it relies so much on mats that it contradicts the reality of self-defense. In my friend's case, he ended up with a serious injury that impacted the rest of his life. Oh, and the only reason his life continued, for the bad guy surely would have beaten him to death, was because there were people that came to his defense.

Think about it: the illogical premises of his wrestling almost killed him - and would have if not for luck. The training he executed to perfection would have killed him. He did what he was supposed to do - what he'd practiced thousands of times - and he nearly died because of it.

That's what we mean.

Being irrational can have serious consequences because reality doesn't care what we think about it. It just is. And we all know this but are skilled truth suppressors. It's our nature.

WE ALL HAVE situations where our common-sense alarm is going off. Gavin DeBecker has a book called *"Gift of Fear"* in which he recommends that as a self-defense tool we listen to our instinctual reticence to some situations. Some of us should have done this before getting married instead of ignoring some red flags. Some of us should have done that before becoming business partners with someone we shouldn't have trusted. And certainly, we should do that with our most basic instinct of self-preservation.

The problem is that, as detailed, we tend to suppress the obvious. The basics of life are altogether clear. We simply have a dreadful tendency to ignore them. Debt. Lust. Anger. The fear of rejection and/or confrontation. Such things often lead us to suppress the obvious.

The previously mentioned Scottish common-sense realism school of philosophy rejected the skepticism of Hume - the brazen contradictions at the root of the philosophical errors we take for granted today. It taught, in short because this is a self-defense book and we've got to get on with it, that common sense presuppositions can be trusted. Much of the damage we're seeing across society, education and politics is because we're claiming to be scientific while simultaneously accepting philosophic nihilism. In other words, common sense be damned because modern academia doesn't believe in objective reality. The alternative is hyper-subjectivism - or, if you will, *my* truth and *your* truth. But a truth that's fully subjective is no truth at all.

The logic of infighting is that the center of mass, neck, throat, jaw and eyes are the primary targets of attack. Simple. Everyone knows this at a common sense level and yet we let *experts* talk us out of it. A thumb in the eye is a frightful tool. A strike to the windpipe isn't something we can generally shrug off. Boxers are often said to have a good or bad chin. A guy that can't take a punch is said to have a glass jaw. A fighter like Tex Cobb, on the other hand, was said to have an iron chin. But who is said to have an iron eyeball? Show me the man with a steel trachea.

Oh, yeah...we all know this but then invest time and training into methods of fighting that simply ignore the obvious. Not only that, but we also ardently oppose any suggestion that this may very well be a dangerous/reckless oversight. The bright lights and vanity of the UFC or professional boxing draws our attention the way that the stunning girl did to me all those years ago and we "forget" the basics. Common sense is shoved out the window and then, even if it's feverishly gripping the ledge, screaming and clawing to climb back in, we take a hammer to its fingers and then lock the window. We don't want to know. We want what we want and what we want is professed as the truth.

For Wing Chun to be a logically valid method of self-defense, as we believe, It must account for these variables. It must have a footwork and balance system that's capable of navigating various terrains.

Check.

It must have a system of striking and moving that's integrated into the footwork scheme.

Check.

It must function in a way that attacks and defends the body's most vulnerable targets.

Check.

And it must have a training system that allows the student to develop tactical reflexes in which this attack and defense scheme is safely tested and improved.

That's Chi-sao. So, *check.*

It must have built-in mechanics and tactics that make it adaptable for use against one or multiple opponents. Furthermore, it must not assume an unarmed opponent. The techniques used must not be dependent upon a strictly man-to-man, unarmed encounter.

Check.

It must not assume mutual combat variables. It must, therefore, have built-in training mechanics and drills that deal with the potential for ambush attacks.

Check.

And, lastly, because self-defense deals with the moral law in regard to violence, a logical martial art must be predicated upon sound moral philosophy including, but not limited to, self-control and respect.

Many other systems fail on one or more of these accounts. Wing Chun, therefore, proves to be a non-contradictory method of self-defense.

Boxing, MMA, BJJ, etc., all fail on multiple counts. They hyper-specialize in single combat (one opponent), with sure footing and borders (ropes, cage, etc.) and eschew the most vulnerable targets in both attack and defense.

A method like Krav Maga addresses these issues, including weapons, and is, therefore, insofar as self-defense goes, more logical than the aforementioned. What it doesn't have is a training system that allows the student to develop tactical/technical reflexes in which close-range combat is safely, but realistically tested. In other words, it has many benefits but it doesn't have Chi-sao. Chi-sao is Wing Chun's ace in the hole. We must close with the obvious, which is that nothing under the sun is perfect. All things have their nature and limits. Our point isn't to say that Wing Chun is the *only* thing that can be logically used for self-defense as that's obviously not the case. Boxers have used their method for years. What we've endeavored to point out is how Wing Chun is the most logically consistent methodology, yet even this conclusion rests upon the reality that it's the individual that uses the system and not the system using the man. If one trains poorly, is out of shape, is half-hearted, and all that...no system can save him.

We will close by reminding the reader that self-defense requires the man as well as the system. The old maxim in Wing Chun is:

First, courage. Second, strength. Third, endurance. Then skill.

. . .

WE WILL ONLY ADD, because space is limited and it's another book for another day, that courage comes from both moral clarity (knowing why you're fighting...the premises of self-defense), and belief in your method. To that end, we've explained both. You know why you have the moral right to self-defense and, also, that Wing Chun, logically trained, is a method you can trust in that jungle of violence.

15

THE PARADOX OF RELAXED AGGRESSION

A big part of Wing Chun and especially Chi-sao is the aspect of using springy energy. This "energy" - or use of structural force - can only be developed through the integration of all aspects of the martial artist. And when we say all aspects, we mean, to borrow the popular saying, mind and body. To say that, though, requires a little explanation due to our culture's rather vacuous abuse of it.

To say mind and body is to admit what's obvious, which is that human beings are integrated beings, not dualistic, but unified. We don't have instincts in the way that we see in the animal kingdom. Everything we need to survive has to be taught to us. One of the most interesting things about mankind is his propensity for self-destruction rather than advancement. Indeed, when we read the Scriptural truth that "there's a way that seems right to a man but its end is death" (Proverbs 16:25) we have before us a fact as plain as day. No lesser mind than Socrates puzzled over the fact that we routinely choose wrong in our attempts to fulfill our desires.

The question is why?

The biblical answer is that man, being integrated, acts from the mind, which is to say, action is guided by thought. A man's basic operating philosophy of life, what he believes is most important, his raison d'être, determines the value, or lack thereof, he places on things. As we think in our heart, so we are (Proverbs 23:7).

In other words, there's always a motive to our action. Always. Often, though, we just don't want to own up to it because it's foolish, contradictory or downright vain.

An immature person often acts as though his/her inner life (his heart/core premises) are a mystery, but it's only thus because they refuse to acknowledge, to themselves and others, the irrationality of those premises. All action taken by a man is that which is consistent with their mind choosing according to their core principles. The problem is that we often don't have the courage to face these principles. Such is, therefore, an incomplete life and it takes training and maturity to overcome this default setting.

Socrates said that an unexamined life isn't one worth living and he was quite correct. Man, being body-mind, lives against his nature when his core premises are set by default. Life is, for all people, a process of thought-action and Socrates' point is that this requires the discipline of self-audit. What's therapy except for a person going to a "professional" to aid in this process? An unexamined life is one in which our core beliefs are taken as a given, that is, mindlessly, which sets off a process of self-denial. A lack of self-audit, of philosophical introspection for a man or woman, is like a bird who won't fly or a lion that won't hunt. We see handicapped people in the world, but the greatest injury and tragedy is the one done to self - it's the dismemberment of mind from body, the slow sawing off of one's faculty of consciousness from their actions. You see evidence of this so dreadfully early when a child is asked why they did the wrong thing and they answer, "I dunno." Deep down they do know, just as we all do. We just don't want to admit that we wanted the wrong thing more than what was right. To admit it terrifies us, so we grow to be masters of truth suppression.

When Jesus said that it's better to enter into life maimed than to go to hell with a healthy body, He was using hyperbole, sure. But the point of the shocking statement is to make us face the truth about our inner life. It's in vogue now to talk about fake news and all that. Fine. But notice the deceit of that statement. To say "fake news" is to claim that truth exists, that it matters, and that it's immoral to lie. That's quite a bit of presumption right there, isn't it? In other words, a person who decries so-called fake news but is himself a moral relativist is a walking contradiction. The greatest fake news of our time is the lie that philosophy and theology don't matter. That itself literally *is philosophy and theology. We simply cannot escape from the responsibility of thinking and forming core values because we are moral beings living in a moral world.*

A very common attempt to evade this responsibility is eastern meditation. For example, the call to "empty our minds" is wrought with contradiction. The Bible calls us to focus our minds in the process of self-audit through the joyful disciplines (and they are disciplines) of prayer and study of Scripture (Isaiah 1:18; Romans 12:1-2). The call to be formless or shapeless is the call to empty ourselves of our humanity and faculty of reason. It's as unnatural as a bird pulling off its wings and trying to drive a car. Man is called, as an integrated being, to *live out his/her core convictions.* This means that belief/faith isn't a feeling as is commonly understood these days. On the contrary, faith, as seen in the Bible, is the absolute agreement with God's evaluation of reality and the commitment to act and live accordingly. We may be inconsistent in doing so, like a boxer in the ring who's trying to establish the jab but can't, but that's not the case. *Faith literally is the act of living an intellectually consistent life.*

Self-audit is that process in which we take our actions and emotional responses and weigh them over against the standards of our core beliefs. Consistency is the mark of maturity. Like getting whacked a lot in sparring, anger, fear, frustration, and all that are calls to deeper self-audit. True life consists of focusing one's mind, not the preposterous attempt to empty it. Freedom isn't the escape from this challenge but the full acceptance of the glorious responsibility of living in integrated consistency. That men lead lives of quiet desperation, as Thoreau said, is because we have black belts in evading the necessities of our true nature.

This is why the attempt to change one's behavior while leaving the core principles in place is a fool's errand. True change starts in the mind/heart and flows to the body. We see this all the time in regard to diet. A person might lose weight for a while and then, inevitably put it right back on. Why? Because the core conviction they hold, the one they don't talk about openly, is that they prefer ease over exercise. What we truly value in our heart is that which we'll choose. Yes, we're capable of altering that process for a time but it's like a man who has his car in *Drive* and then gets out and starts pushing it backwards. He can do it. It takes incredible effort. It's exhausting exactly because the car isn't in gear and eventually, despite the toil, he's going to go back the other way.

So, we choose wrong things because our core belief is at odds with reality. The short of it is that we face a sea of particular facts in life and must interpret their meaning. To do so requires a basic operating standard. One's evaluation of any particular fact is dependent upon their core belief about reality. This accounts for why arguments about politics are often so futile. The contestants aren't actually debating about the policy or candidate so much as they're arguing *past* each other in terms of government philosophy. If you're prone to avoid such debates because you see them as unhelpful and something akin to watching pigs sling mud at one another, you're half right.

You see, pigs oinking it out in a mud pit is as useless an endeavor as trying to change someone's mind about a core philosophy through debate of an auxiliary issue. One's fundamental belief directs their interpretive faculty, which is to say it gives the all-important context to every fact they encounter.

This is what the Bible means when it says, "don't rely on your own understanding, but in all your ways acknowledge God and He'll make straight your paths (Proverbs 3:5-6)." In other words, the key to seeing reality without contradiction, as it truly is, is to start with the correct presupposition. To see God as preeminent in one's chain of reasoning colors how all other facts are seen. For example, following this line of thought, one would come to a question about ethics and ask, "what does the Bible say (Romans 4:3)?" If God is the source of all things then He'd be the final standard of appeal, right? The goal, therefore, is to be as consistent to that standard as possible in judging the individual facts of life. Intellectual consistency is the goal.

All conflict is a result of inconsistency. Contradictions are evidence of flaws in theory or failures of integrated performance.

The reason we encounter so much internal conflict - that is, emotional traumas - is because of intellectual contradiction. Since mankind isn't a robot, nor some other kind of automaton, he must live in God's world according to principles and structures superimposed upon him. Mankind is a derivative, not original; man is no god; he's a re-creator, never creator. This means that man's burden is to seek truth (theoretical) and then act upon it (action/practice). This is what mind-body means. Any contradiction will lead to leaks in one's behavioral performance. Tension/stress is a result of contradiction; relaxation/contentment is the product of thinking rightly about reality. The goal isn't to "empty the mind" but to rightly understand reality and then learn to act in accordance with that correct knowledge.

Think of it this way: if you're having a problem with being too tense while doing Chi-sao the tension is a product of mind and/or body, right? Initially, when you first begin, your body won't know the techniques and this vacuum will cause you to be tense. Once you know the techniques and have had time to get better you should be able to perform with springy aggression. If that's not the case then the only culprit for the tension would be an intellectual error at the root of the person doing the technique.

Here are some common errors of thought that infect our performance.

THINKING *you should never be hit - or perfectionism.* This irrational presumption puts emotional tension on you right from the get-go. Instead of flowing and letting your skill work for you, you'll be preoccupied with not making mistakes. Any mistake will mean, according to your presumption, that you failed and since this is such an irrational standard it will cause you physical tension. The technique is merely following suit, so to speak. Emotions aren't mysteries; they're the outworking of one's premises.

Emotions are simply one's philosophy of life in action.

A person who's seeking perfection rather than skill has committed a serious theological blunder. Only God is ontologically perfect, so that category (perfection), or level of attainment, is impossible for mankind. Men and women can achieve great skill in their performance, but not perfection. The biblical doctrine of glorifying God is seen in this apparent conundrum. Letting go of the contradiction of perfection allows one to see reality aright and focus on performance skill.

The false ideal of perfectionism is the coin of egotism. Heads, and it's the sin of pride; tails and it's the fear of not being perfect. One guy is arrogant and the other is seen as insecure. In truth, both are too self-focused. They misidentify to goal of life/reality and nature of mankind. We're always in the process of actualization. Christian philosophy calls this process sanctification. It means that man is moving toward their potential and, this is critical, *working toward the glorious goal of living up to the reality of the truth they've come to know.* Perfectionism in any variant is a denial of this reality and puts one at odds with the truth. It places oneself as the possessor of ontological perfection, at the pinnacle; it sees man as the goal rather than God. Perfectionism denies that man is a pilgrim in this lifetime.

EXTREMES IN PERSONALITY *rather than balanced skill.*

Living in a fallen world (again assuming the biblical standard as the logical definition of why we exist and "what for?") we're all faced with a serious challenge. We don't like to talk about it much but it's always there. What happens is that we're always trying to make ourselves "arrive" when, in fact, this is logically impossible. No person on earth is ever fully "actualized" because that would mean there's nothing else to learn, no changes needed, no room for growth. On one level we certainly know this. No person would be so bold as to say that they've completely mastered this or that, much less life itself. No one would blurt out, "hey, you rubes, I've got nothing left to learn...come and adore me!"

Though we aren't that brazenly irrational that doesn't mean we don't, in fact, hide the desire for actualization in our hearts. *This is precisely where frustration comes from - it's the emotional response to the intellectual mistake of believing in one's own deity.* I know...I know... that's a big statement and it's hard to hear. But when we encounter frustration we're running headlong into the obvious fact that reality doesn't change for us, we must adapt to it. Unresolved fear and/or frustration turns to bitterness.

In the case of martial arts, the desire to not have to change, to be *utterly safe,* explains why we see schools where no one uses any serious forward pressure during Chi-sao. Or it explains why there's a cult of personality around the hero instructor - he/she becomes the lodestar and the students/disciples don't have to bother themselves with truly growing, only imitating the master. Or it's why there are no-touch KO schools; internal energy nonsense and all that.

You might be highly aggressive. If so, you try and find an outlet for it that allows you to maximize that aggression without having to become more balanced. It's the Cobra-Kai issue. Or you go the other way if you're passive. You see people using lots of pressure and force in their Chi-sao and think it's barbaric. I see folks who think like that on my YouTube page when they comment that I'm only teaching external Wing Chun and eschewing the true, inner truths.

In point of fact, this is the inner truth - and that's that one's core convictions always direct their actions. The attempt to somehow tap into some mysterious form of inner power is the attempt to make an end-around of God's reality. But like all such attempts, it's like handing a football in an NFL game to a toddler. The non-sensical notion of "inner martial arts" actually, in the end, denies the true nature of the power of the integrated mind and body. It's another sad example of man amputating himself - in this case, cutting off the body to allegedly free it.

There was a scene in a movie, *Demolition Man,* where Sylvester Stallone's character, who is living in the future (I'd explain but go ahead and watch it for yourself...it's hilarious), is about to have sex with the character played delightfully by Sandra Bullock. Stallone is predictably excited as she goes to get ready - presumably to change into something more comfortable as the saying goes. What happens, however, is that she comes out with some kind of virtual reality gizmo they're both supposed to wear for the "sex." As Stallone finds out, to his great dismay, is that sex in the hyper-sanitized future involves the fantasy rather than the reality. It's mind-to-mind rather than actual physical intimacy. He rejects the whole thing altogether.

As satire of the political correctness movement in the 90's, which grew into our current woke totalitarianism, this was quite funny. But it's also apropos here. It illustrates the foolishness of separating mind-body.

The extremes of personality are something that literally every single one of us faces. Systematic skill, gained through disciplined practice, frees us from these extremes – whether of overconfidence or great fear. In all my years of teaching I've never seen anyone fail who committed themselves to the discipline. Likewise, I've never seen anyone succeed who failed to commit to it. Because we're all imperfect and finite, that is to say, imperfect, we need disciplined instruction and practice. This doesn't come right away and we can't rush it.

THE GREAT CHALLENGE of Chi-sao is that it's both aggressive and relaxed. It challenges us to be structurally powerful while springy and adaptable. High level performance in Wing Chun causes us to confront our contradictions and irrational extremes. Being aggressive is good if balanced by good form and springiness; being passive is good if it means we've learned to snappily counter aggressive mistakes. One's personality will still be there, but it will be "rounded out" by the skill of Wing Chun. Yet, the system can't do it all by itself. We must apply ourselves to the great task of clear thinking. Contradictions in our theory, if allowed to fester, will choke off real skill.

Also, the refusal to accept the correction that comes via the drill - getting hit, losing control, etc. - will lead invariably to playing Chi-sao in a vacuum. Done right, however, it's a glorious thing and the Chi-sao student will learn how to be frightfully aggressive while controlling their opponent with springy technique. Having no way as way is, by this understanding, a process of integration of mind and body rather than an irrational mystery.

NOTES

3. The Drill

1. Wing Chun doesn't equate to all-out fighting either, by the way. All training is exactly that: training. It must, by the law of logical inference, be consensual, so it can't be self-defense fighting since choice is involved. What we're talking about is the ability to use drills that have the highest degree of logical coherence with the facts of reality even though they aren't reality themselves.

5. Simultaneous Attack & Defense - Lin Siu Daai Da

1. I have no problem with Ms. Rand's emphasis on liberty and reason, only upon her staunch atheism. The "fatal" flaw, or contradiction in her systematic is in her metaphysic. If everything that is simply is by accident, and there's no ultimate Person causing everything, then what is is arbitrary. Her systematic could never make sense of why, if man is the animal of reason, and reason is man's nature, the majority are unreasonable. Biblical Christianity explains this. Mankind has a moral rebellion problem that influences its intellect according to the Biblical philosophy and that makes sense of why men are so tragically prone to self-destructive tendencies and error.
2. We must remind the reader that systems and methods don't apply themselves. The structures and principles of a system are applied by people who have varying degrees of physical attributes, skill, intelligence, and aggression and composure under pressure.

6. Thermal Exhaust Port

1. Eric Lilleor, the magnificent editor-in-chief of Wing Chun Illustrated, said it perfectly: "Skill is something that's learnable. Talent is the rate at which you can acquire a particular skill."

7. Chi-Sao & Grappling

1. This is a wonderful way of understanding what's called in theology proper, the *creature-Creator distinction*. Because man is not God, his work and training are necessary aspects of his existence. Being a derivative being, not the necessary and original Being, man's labor brings him to greater skill. Training and educa-

tion are aspects of the creature (man) who is *becoming*. Man is a part of reality and is always tasked with having to adapt to it, which requires the application of his mind (reason) and training to bring forth logically consistent action.

ACKNOWLEDGMENTS

Donald Grey Barnhouse wrote: "When a man becomes prosperous through the efforts of another, usually his first reaction is to push his benefactor aside. Pride claims all credit and thinks it demeaning to give credit to another. The common effect of prosperity is to harden the heart...". To this, Barnhouse recommended that we focus on humility and gratitude as primary qualities in life. He said, "Phone or write someone today and thank him for what he has done for you. Lord, bring to mind kindnesses that should be acknowledged."

With that said, your author must admit that he's been guilty in the past of a critical spirit and ungrateful heart. It's something of which I'm certainly ashamed, watchful for at present, and thankful for the grace of God.

I recall at one sorry time when I was quite frustrated by my lack of professional progress in life, back in 1996, how I bitterly complained to a family member during a long drive from New York back to South Carolina. I was convinced that I deserved more in life. I was upset that I was working 50-60 hours a week at what I saw as a dead-end job just to support a fledgling martial arts school that was losing money. My bitter heart was convinced of what I was owed. I said ugly things. I whined like a child, though I was supposed to be a grown man and a leader (obviously I wasn't yet). I report this to you for the simple reason that I've seen over the years the damage that lack of gratitude does to us personally as well as to our relationships. With that said, I'd like to follow the good Mr. Barnhouse's advice and, in the Lord, thank many that have been helpful to me upon my walk.

Also, it's to report that until I fully engaged the battle against entitlement and bitterness I never saw true success. By the grace of God I came to know that all of my life, talents, and opportunities were from the Lord anyway...all of it, everything. It's also to inform the reader of a critical lesson I've learned through this process of sanctification/maturation and that is that ungratefulness is the root of so much conflict. A martial artist dedicated to peace simply can't be bitter and entitled because that means he/she moves only from one conflict to the next in life. It's like a fireman who's also a part-time arsonist.

To that end I'd like to thank not only the obvious folks I've thanked before in my books but some others who have certainly contributed to the martial artist I am today.

My brother, Micheal, who was the one who introduced me to Wing Chun back in 1981. Micheal was my first Sifu even though he was learning himself. An artist and photographer by trade and calling, Michael taught me to see life as not only a Kung-fu man but also as an artist. I remember a spectacular day, in fact, that encapsulated it perfectly. It was February 24, 1985, an unseasonably warm and glorious day - especially in upstate New York where I grew up. Michael was in town for the weekend (he's 11 years older and had recently finished his undergrad work at RIT) and along with several of my friends - big, goofy Colin especially - we did Chi-sao for hours over at the park. We trained and laughed and got smacked around and ate lots of pizza. It was glorious and I remember sitting there as the sun was getting low and dreaming of being able to do that for a living. Michael planted those Kung-fu seeds, watered them, encouraged them, and I'm forever grateful.

Sifu Dan was my private Wing Chun instructor in upstate New York once I was old enough to drive. He was/is a very private man who didn't want a commercial school. I was able to learn from him due to knowing someone who introduced me to him. He didn't want teenage boys (I was 18) as students, finding them flaky and immature. I resembled that, of course. Nevertheless, I won him over, he later reported, with my goofiness and dedication. He imparted to me the necessity of strength through structure. Respecting his privacy, I'll refrain from saying much else while thanking him profusely for all he taught me.

I'd also like to thank the incredible Greenville Academy family. We've spent countless hours not just training, but laughing, sharing, and talking. Aaron and Devin, featured in this book, are two of the most extraordinary men I've ever met. Devoted to the Lord Jesus Christ, wonderful fathers and husbands, and great artists too. Their friendship has meant so much to me over the years. The fact that men of their character are in my life tells me that I'm doing something right.

The Academy family has been growing since I first got to Greenville in July of 1994, all young and passionate and full of dreams. Rusty Starkey was the first person I trained to advanced and instructor level, having started with me in 1995. He later went on to train several amateur MMA champions in his own school. He was best man at my wedding in 1999 and has been a true blessing over the years.

I'd also like to acknowledge Mark Strickland who doesn't get a chance to train with us so much anymore because he has 3,000 children (maybe a little bit of an exaggeration). Mark is one of the funniest and most sincere people I've ever met. Like our Lord said of Nathanael (John 1:47), Mark is a man in whom there's no deceit. He's as honest a soul as I've ever met. Moreover, putting him and Aaron together on a long ride in the Tundra is some of the best entertainment in the world. Those two guys arguing about movies is sincerely some of the funniest stuff I've ever heard. I've lost weight due to laughing so hard.

Jim Quast, who teaches up in Minnesota - where summer lasts from June 21st to June 22nd - always amazed me with how dedicated he was, not only to Wing Chun, but also to his beloved daughters. What a man! Jesse Moshure, who like Quast moved north, in his case to the frozen land of cheese (Wisconsin), is a great Wing Chun man. Though they aren't in Greenville anymore, they're not forgotten.

James Shoeni is a wonderful artist/photographer and Wing Chun man. Some of my favorite moments have been talking art with him after classes. He sees Wing Chun through the eyes of the artist (a little like Devin Smith and my brother, Michael) and spending time with him always brings a smile to my heart. James is a truly humble soul.

I've already acknowledged Wes Childers in a previous book, but it bears repeating. He's a joyous force of life and true friend. There are also some tremendous long time students who should be included in future books: David and Glenn, only seen here getting smacked (a point we've had some chuckles over), Beth and Kevin. And definitely Seanna...a picture perfect example of perseverance and humility.

There are so many more I could mention...so many wonderful souls that have enriched my life and to whom I give great thanks to God. I pray that He keeps me humble and my heart soft, always heeding His instruction and correction.

ABOUT THE AUTHOR

Jason Korol is the author of over a dozen books and regular columnist for the world's leading Wing Chun magazine, *Wing Chun Illustrated*. Originally from Upstate New York and now living, writing and teaching in South Carolina, he's one of the world's leading authorities on self-defense and its moral implications. If you're interested in contacting him to learn more about his teachings and methods, please go to Greenvilleacademy.com.

ALSO BY JASON KOROL

Wing Chun for the Modern Warrior

Wing Chun's Art of War: Chum Kiu

Wing Chun Wooden Dummy

Wing Chun's Foundation: Siu Lim Tao

JKD's Way of the Blade

JKD Infighting

Wing Chun Applications: From the School to the Street

Jeet Kune Do Foundations

Christ & Self-Defense: How God Solves the Problem of Violence

Also in Fiction:

The Undefeated